Closing the LEADERSHIP GAP

The authors dedicate this book to educational leaders in schools and universities who are searching for exemplary field-tested methods for preparing new leaders who can address the current realities of the educational environment and build the leadership capacity of their organizations in order to improve individual and overall student and staff performance.

Closing the LEADERSHIP GAP

How District and University Partnerships Shape Effective School Leaders

TERESA N. MILLER
MARY DEVIN
ROBERT J. SHOOP

A JOINT PUBLICATION

For information:

Corwin Press
A Sage Publications Company
2455 Teller Road
Thousand Oaks, California 91320
www.corwinpress.com

Sage Publications Ltd.
1 Oliver's Yard
55 City Road
London EC1Y 1SP
United Kingdom

Sage Publications India Pvt. Ltd.
B 1/I 1 Mohan Cooperative
Industrial Area
Mathura Road, New Delhi 110 044
India

Sage Publications Asia-Pacific Pte. Ltd.
33 Pekin Street #02-01
Far East Square
Singapore 048763

Printed in the United States of America.

Library of Congress Cataloging-in-Publication Data

Miller, Teresa N.
Closing the leadership gap: How district and university partnerships shape effective school leaders / Teresa N. Miller, Mary Devin, and Robert J. Shoop.
p. cm.
Includes bibliographical references and index.
ISBN 978-1-4129-3674-3 (cloth)
ISBN 978-1-4129-3675-0 (pbk.)
1. School administrators—Training of—United States. 2. Educational leadership—United States. 3. College-school cooperation—United States. I. Devin, Mary. II. Shoop, Robert J. III. Title.
LB1738.5.S56 2007
371.2'011—dc22

2006101260

This book is printed on acid-free paper.

07 08 09 10 11 10 9 8 7 6 5 4 3 2 1

Acquisitions Editor: Elizabeth Brenkus
Editorial Assistants: Desirée Enayati and Ena Rosen
Production Editor: Melanie Birdsall
Copy Editor: Carla Freeman
Typesetter: C&M Digitals (P) Ltd.
Proofreader: Gail Fay
Indexer: Naomi Linzer
Cover Designer: Michael Dubowe
Graphic Designer: Lisa Riley

Contents

About the Authors

Teresa N. Miller is an associate professor at Kansas State University in the Department of Educational Leadership, serving as a coliaison for site-based leadership academies training prospective principals and teacher leaders. Prior to coming to KSU, she was a public school educator for 28 years, as a teacher of language arts, gifted education facilitator, and principal at both elementary and secondary levels. As a principal, she received the Excellence in Educational Leadership Award from the University Council for Educational Administration and was actively involved in her district in the planning and development of Professional Development Schools, a university–public school partnership for preparing teachers.

Mary Devin has been an elementary teacher, library media specialist, director of public information, and chief business official. In the last 12 of her 37 years in school administration, she was superintendent of a very diverse, mobile, high-poverty district that became one of the highest academic performers in the state. Under her leadership, the district partnered often with a university, implementing academies to prepare administrators and to build teacher leadership capacity. Dr. Devin is an associate professor at Kansas State University in the Department of Educational Leadership, and serves as coliaison for leadership academies.

Robert J. Shoop has been a professor at Kansas State University and Senior Scholar in the Leadership Studies program since 1976. Prior to coming to Kansas State, he was a public school teacher, a school administrator, and an evaluator of state department of education programs. He is the recipient of the Outstanding Graduate Professor and the Outstanding Undergraduate Professor awards at Kansas State. Dr. Shoop is a nationally recognized forensic expert in the area of school law and risk management. He is the author or coauthor of 17 books and over 100 journal articles, monographs, and book chapters, and has produced six award-winning educational video programs.

Acknowledgments

We are grateful for the ongoing research efforts related to preparing educational leaders by Linda Lambert, Michael Fullan, Mid-continent Research Education and Learning (McREL), Leithwood and Associates, Southern Regional Education Board (SREB), University Council of Educational Administration (UCEA), and many others.

In our own institution, we are grateful to our dean, department chair, and colleagues within the College of Education for their forward thinking, guidance, collaboration, and creativity in the design and development of customized academies for preparing educational leaders; to the district-level administrators who have partnered with us to create a new model for collaborative partnerships; and to our students who have so willingly engaged in these efforts and exceeded all of our expectations. We are also grateful for the Professional Development School model at our university that has served as a foundation for our university–public school partnerships and enhanced our efforts. As a result, we have been able to develop a simultaneous-growth model that partners universities and schools to prepare educational leaders who are steeped in both theory and practice and have programs that are rigorous and engaging, and in which all partners share benefits that last far beyond the initial training programs.

Corwin Press gratefully acknowledges the contributions of the following individuals:

Kathy Grover, Assistant Superintendent
Clever R-V Public Schools
Clever, MO

Susan M. Landt, Assistant Professor
St. Norbert College
De Pere, WI

Jim Lentz, Superintendent
USD 402 Augusta Public Schools
Augusta, KS

Timothy D. Letzring, Chair and Associate Professor
Leadership and Counselor Education
University of Mississippi
University, MS

Gina Marx, Assistant Superintendent
USD 262 Valley Center
Valley Center, KS

Vicki Vaughn, Principal
Edgelea Elementary School
Lafayette, IN

Susan Villani, Senior Program Research Associate
Learning Innovations at WestEd
Woburn, MA

Richard Yee, Principal
Oster Elementary School
San Jose, CA

Introduction

We are three veteran educators who have taken separate paths to arrive at a common position: The greatest challenge facing education today is preparing quality educational leaders for our schools—leaders who can thrive in the high-stakes-accountability environment that exists today. Our vision of leadership has become more inclusive in its scope, and we acknowledge that school leadership preparation programs of past years will not produce the results needed for the future. We see the preparation of school leaders as a responsibility extending far beyond the university and state credentialing bodies. This responsibility extends to all educators, those in the university, within schools, and within each state. We hope our collaborative efforts to share our thoughts and experiences here will help others who have similar concerns and a willingness to explore new ventures to address them.

Each of us began our careers in education as teachers in public school settings. Together, we have served at all levels: elementary, middle, and high school. As administrators, we have been assistant principals, principals at various levels, school improvement leaders, and superintendents. We bring a variety of school experiences to this topic of preparing leaders—those of a superintendent of a very diverse, mobile, high-poverty district with high student academic performance; a K–12 principal actively involved in professional development school partnerships; and a cofounder of a rapidly expanding program of leadership studies, who is also a recognized expert in guiding school personnel in school law and risk management. Our experiences in "the real world" are fresh in our minds. Presently, all three of us are members of the Department of Educational Leadership at a major university, preparing administrators for schools in our state and beyond. Graduates of our programs are currently serving in a variety of leadership positions, within and outside our state. This book is written from our personal perspectives, but we hope the reader will keep in mind that these opinions are founded in the collection of firsthand, reality-based experiences we have shared with our current and past school partners for the last 15 years.

University preparation programs for educational leaders are not infrequently criticized for lack of connectedness to the real world—creating an alleged gap between theory and practice. We readily admit that the traditional approach to preparing educational leaders no longer produces the results we are looking for in our own university program. However, we are excited about the great potential we have encountered when school and university leaders combine their talents to design better ways of developing leaders. Partnerships focusing on organizational and program redesign and restructuring have the potential to create a renaissance in the preparation of educational leaders that renews and revitalizes both organizational systems.

We believe there is a need to move from thinking about preparation as the sole responsibility of those charged with discovering and preserving research and theory (universities) to a vision of preparation as a shared partnership between theorists and those who must make things work in the real world (current practitioners in the field). The philosophical foundation of our view on educational leadership is this: No matter what position you hold—teacher, principal, superintendent, university professor, support staff, or community leader—preparing school leaders is YOUR responsibility. It will take all of us, working together, to best prepare those who must lead our schools tomorrow—and, literally, the need begins tomorrow! The challenges are before our schools now. As an unexpected bonus, we discovered that this professional growth in leadership happens not only for the students in the program but also for the current leaders who become directly involved in planning and delivering the partnership model.

We know we are not the only ones who have these concerns or are engaged in efforts to make meaningful changes to preparation programs. Indeed, we have learned much from conference presentations and published accounts describing efforts under way in other locations. Across the country, many university faculties have been working to improve preparation programs for years. We are indebted to those who have shared their personal experiences with professional colleagues. Publications and conferences sponsored by the University Council for Educational Administration (UCEA) and recent well-publicized analyses of current programs provide pertinent information for those directly charged with responsibility for preparing educational leaders at the building and district levels. Our purpose here is not to argue the need for change, nor is it our intent to imply that our programs are the only examples of successful change under way. Readers who wish to delve further into various approaches to change will not find it difficult to locate the information.

Our purpose here is to share what we have learned from the opportunities we have had working in a university environment where leaders are open to new ideas for improving service and are willing to adjust operational structures to allow for change. Our good fortune included finding public school leaders and building-level practitioners willing to work with us as partners in making substantial changes in practice. We share our experiences, offering them as another source of information that might be helpful to all who share responsibility for and care about preparing effective, quality leaders for our schools.

This book offers a challenge to educators such as the following:

- University leaders currently involved in administrator preparation programs who want to develop and strengthen program connections to real schools and increase their ability to blend theory with real-world practices. Our message is that it can be done.
- School leaders who desire to build the leadership capacity of their organizations by developing both practicing and prospective leaders with a strong foundation in both theory and practice. Our message is that by working together, we can build that leadership capacity.
- Practitioners looking for something beyond preservice preparation, who want to grow professionally and continue to develop leadership skills that can contribute to success in a high-stakes-accountability world. Our message is that through a partnership model, we can prepare exemplary leaders for that world.

We begin by describing how our vision of educational leadership has evolved, briefly touching on some of the information that contributed to the change. Our goal is to offer a program based on an effective blend of theory and practice; a program designed by collaborative partnerships; and a program that produces an integrated, spiraling curriculum emphasizing ethical leadership performance. We include insights from university professors, public school leaders, and leaders-in-training who support the importance of and need for this approach to leadership development. Because the positive impact of leadership upon student achievement and the strength of public school–university partnerships have been documented by other researchers, we identify those key components we have chosen to include in our partnership experiences. The book concludes with a detailed description of a successful university–district partnership, complete with planning tools that can be used by others interested in similar partnership models. We know it can work—we have experienced it firsthand and are continuing to develop new partnerships.

We have organized our message in the following manner:

- *Chapter 1* provides reasons for changing the way we think about leadership. We recognize that university and public school partners must play active roles in the preparation process if we are to develop leaders who can build the leadership capacity of their own stakeholders and thrive as knowledgeable, ethical, caring leaders for schools, for all students, and for themselves.

- *Chapter 2* provides a new vision of leadership, beginning with a new look at practice and a reanalysis of our expectations of school leadership today. We live in a time of rapid change. Successful leaders must be able to apply leadership theory to what is happening in schools today. Traditional programs must be updated to reflect the radical changes in practice and the present challenges facing school leaders.

- *Chapter 3* delineates the theoretical basis for producing collaborative, caring, inclusive leaders. Important dimensions of leadership theory are identified and described that continue to be necessary components for any leadership preparation program.

- *Chapter 4* defines why traditional preparation programs for leaders that emphasize theory over practice no longer work. Collaborative partnerships between universities and school districts must become the new model for preparing successful future leaders: programs where practice guides theory and theory informs practice.

- *Chapter 5* describes the rethinking and redesigning process for the curriculum to prepare educational leaders. In a collaboratively designed, integrated, spiraling curriculum, university staff and public school leaders jointly participate as teachers for and learners with leaders-in-training.

- *Chapter 6* specifies ethics as a core dimension of leadership. Community expectations continue to hold educational leaders to a high standard. This chapter defines and describes the emphasis on ethical leadership included in our preparation programs as a response to today's global environment and emerging reports of corporate and government corruption.

- *Chapter 7* relates the story of a collaborative university–public school partnership, based on the authors' own experiences of developing nontraditional preparation programs, in partnership with public schools, to more effectively prepare school leaders. Examples of tools used in our partnerships are included in the "Resources" section.

1

A Change in the Way We Think About Leadership

We need fundamental changes in the cultures of organizations and systems . . . leaders working to change conditions, including the development of other leaders to reach a critical mass.

—M. Fullan (2005)

It happens to us all, whatever our roles. We look to the future, trying our best to make wise decisions, only to find ourselves staring into widespread, frustrating uncertainties. Dilemmas like this are known as *long-fuse, big-bang* problems. Whatever direction we choose to take could play out with a big bang—career disillusionment, student failure, and increased ethnic and racial fragmentation. It can take years to learn whether the decisions we make today are wise or not. Even more disheartening, the long-fuse, big-bang questions don't lend themselves to simple solutions. However, we must make some decisions, and we must make them now. We cannot wait for certainty to appear. Since it is impossible to know how the future will play out, the goal is to discover a robust strategy that allows for uncertainties.

NOTE: Material from Ivory, G., & Acker-Hocevar, M. (2005), *Voices From the Field: Phase 3* (Superintendent focus group interview transcripts), Austin, TX: University Council for Educational Administration, is used with permission.

Our university's educational leadership department has an extensive history of working with local districts to prepare the best leaders possible for today's environment of diverse needs and high-stakes accountability. We believe that the relationship between new school leaders and their home universities should continue throughout their careers. Consequently, we developed a preparation program in cooperation with outstanding practicing school leaders and university faculty. This program has continued to be modified as it became obvious that there were increasing concerns about the future availability of qualified school leaders.

Superintendents' concerns included finding ways to better prepare prospective school leaders for the challenges of rising expectations, reduced financial resources, increasing diversity, and decreasing community support as the future becomes increasingly murky and embedded in accountability. Based on personal experiences as recent public school administrators and as current students of leadership theory and research, we began rethinking who needed to be included in this search for answers. It was clear that those interested in the preparation of quality school leaders do not work just in universities. Our experience affirms the value of joining practicing school leaders and university faculty to plan for this uncertain future.

Our leadership preparation program was designed by the university staff authorized to prepare school leaders, practicing district leaders who will employ new leaders, practicing building leaders who will rely on the newcomers as peer colleagues, and the teaching ranks from which prospective leaders-in-training will come. The successful interaction of all four of these sources is the ultimate measure of successful leadership.

In this chapter, we review the events that led us to this point of inviting others to become active partners in preparing school leaders. We introduce four scenarios, featuring personalities that we will refer to from time to time throughout the book. These scenarios illustrate the four critical elements of the planning process: the professor (university), the chief school administrator (school district leader), the building administrator (school building leader), and a teacher (prospective leader-in-training). These characters are fictional composites inspired by real people from our past partnerships and the authentic interests they brought to our conversations. As you read the scenarios, imagine, if you will, that the four are occurring simultaneously in different locations—which is quite close to what actually took place.

The scenarios illustrate the world of uncertainty facing current educational leaders and prospective leaders-in-training. Each story features a representative of one of the four critical players. Each of these critical players has a personal stake in the outcome: a need to be addressed. Each also brings resources, understanding of current conditions, and a contribution to the vision of quality school leadership. In the following pages, we will discuss some of the dynamics that shape the collective future of these four key players. If you are reading this book, it is quite likely that you are one of our four central players. As you read the scenarios, feel free to add your own personal details to the description that most closely resembles your role in the process of preparing leaders.

The University

Professor Scatain was in his office reviewing the notes from his last site visit with Sally Yarley, one of his first-year principals. The new licensure guidelines required him to visit four times this year, and his first visit had been disturbing. Despite his best intentions, he was afraid that Sally was not adequately prepared for what she was facing. Scatain had advised Sally to take this job, with its challenges, but now he was not so sure that it had been wise counsel or that even he himself would be up to the challenges. In the assigned high school, student performance was below adequate yearly progress (AYP) proficiency standards and had been for two years, which meant that serious steps needed to be taken. Sally's administrative contract for the second year hinged on having her school make AYP this year in both reading and math. Her student population included several minority groups, none of which had met the AYP standards. As Professor Scatain had talked with Sally yesterday, he sensed that she remembered the Interstate School Leaders Licensure Consortium (ISLLC) standards and programs and systems to support them but that now she really needed strategies for putting them into place quickly—in order to address her school's unique problems—or she would likely be out of a job. In his education classes, Scatain had talked boldly of problem solving, and the students had generated solutions for multiple scenarios that he had developed from his own experiences, but he now saw that his artificial situations did not realistically portray the current conditions that Sally and his other students were facing. Professor Scatain realized that he needed a stronger connection with the public schools in order to better prepare his students as educational leaders. He wondered whether his friend, Superintendent DeBoyce, of a nearby district, would be interested in a partnership to help improve the university's administrator preparation program.

The Public School District Leader

Superintendent DeBoyce looked over the district's list of current administrators, and she noted that nearly two thirds of the names listed were eligible for retirement in the next five years. With new economic growth in the community, she knew that there would be a great need for new leadership in the district, and she wanted to help train these individuals. In her 20 years as superintendent, she had watched many changes come and go, but she was greatly concerned about the impact of the current high-stakes-accountability atmosphere on district programs. Having recently hired two new administrators, she was disappointed that they seemed unprepared to meet the challenges of this politically charged environment. The candidates had come highly recommended, equipped with strong research backgrounds, but they seemed to lack the skills and knowledge to lead a staff in changing traditional practices in order to improve student performance. These applicants were also unaware that their middle-class-advantaged experiences were very dissimilar to those of the students in their buildings, and they did not seem to know where to find the needed resources. Frustrated, Superintendent DeBoyce picked up the phone to call one of her former professors, Professor Scatain, to see whether they could work together to develop a plan that would prepare administrators for this new environment—leaders who could build the leadership capacity of the entire system.

The Public School Building Leader

Principal Yarley looked through the small window of her office. She enjoyed watching the student life as she worked on her building report for the year. As she completed the information, she realized that she had learned quite a bit on this, her first year as a new principal of an elementary school, but she had learned most of it on the job. She planned to have a talk with the major professor of her doctoral program next week to review some items she thought would be beneficial for students like her, who wanted to become quality principals. First of all, she would tell him that he needed to spend a lot more time teaching students ways to help staff members get along and work together to improve student performance. Sally was still amazed at how often she'd been called upon to mediate all kinds of issues—between and among students, staff members, parents, community members, and even those who supervised her at the central office—and someone could have prepared her better for the 24/7 demands on her time. Now that she had finished the first year, she did have a better idea about ways she could streamline those demands, but it would have helped if some hints about such demands had been given during her studies, as well as ideas about prioritizing and time management. Her students had made some progress as their teachers focused on improving math and reading scores, but she was not sure about the next steps to continue that progress. As Principal Yarley finished up the report, she also made a note for Professor Scatain about public appearances, especially with the board members. She knew she would be grilled when she presented this information: Their enrollment was declining and so were the test scores, especially for the special education students, and she would have to be ready for all their questions. They had worked hard as a whole building, but the results didn't show yet, and it would probably take three years for all their efforts to result in higher test scores. As she looked out the window again, she realized that it was 8 p.m. and she was alone in the building. She had missed dinner and her daughter's soccer game. She quickly added "finding balance" to the list for Professor Scatain.

The Leader-in-Training

Karl Weiss perused the brochure from the university about the master's program in educational administration. He noted the classes and the length of time required, and considered his schedule. He had been teaching English for seven years at Midvale Middle School and sponsored the "Science Olympiad" students. His administrator had often suggested that he consider administration, and he was interested because he thought he could do a better job than some current administrators. He had previously asked about support from the district as to whether he should consider taking classes toward building licensure. The response was less than he expected—no release time, though his principal had offered moral support. Karl took an education class last summer and had not been impressed with the textbook applications as to what school life was like. The information seemed way out of date, and he wondered whether the administrator preparation program was any different. He thought about his students and realized that though he was trying to do all he could to help them, he often provided too much help, and he wanted to learn how to help students develop leadership and independence skills. He had asked colleagues for assistance, but they were not much help and had few suggestions. Two of them told him that if he waited long enough, the No Child Left Behind requirements would "go away." They were almost ready to retire and were not as concerned as he was about student performance. He stopped by the main office on his way home and picked up a colorful brochure from his mailbox. The brochure described a new partnership for leadership training that was a cooperative effort of the school district and the local university. The timing of the brochure with his own interests was perfect. Karl decided to apply.

Each of these four players has a key role in the process of training educational leaders. The leadership preparation model presented in this book recognizes that each player must be actively involved in the partnership, by collaborative planning, implementation, and evaluation of the training program. This model also respects the unique perspectives and experiences each player brings to the process. This chapter defines the educational landscape for today's educators; the ineffectiveness of traditional programs; the increasing challenges facing educators today, along with the emerging research; and suggestions for addressing the obstacles that exist in both universities and schools.

THE EDUCATIONAL LANDSCAPE

The educational landscape and the world for new administrators has changed dramatically since 2001, when the No Child Left Behind Act of 2001 (NCLB) went into effect, with its emphasis on requiring *individual* student performance at a proficiency level and serious sanctions placed upon schools that did not meet that standard. This high-stakes accountability for each student is very different from the previous expectation for schools to do their best for *most* of the students, with no real accountability.

Just as the problems facing school leaders have multiplied exponentially, the number of educators wishing to take steps toward school leadership is dwindling rapidly. An estimated 40% of school administrators across the nation are expected to retire by 2005 (Ferrandino & Tirozzi, 2000, as cited in Gustafson, 2005, p. 1). Many administrators are taking advantage of early-out options. Across the nation, there are enough licensed administrators to fill all positions, but many are choosing not to serve. As the tuition costs and testing requirements increase, fewer educators are choosing the administrative route—many opt to stay in the classroom, and others leave education altogether. Due to the comparatively low salaries for teachers and administrators, especially in light of the increased responsibilities, many qualified administrators are selecting more lucrative, less politically stressful careers.

Additional reasons cited for the looming shortage of quality administrative candidates include the following: not feeling prepared for the type of work now required, societal issues, lack of support, polarized cultures, and increased accountability (Cusick, 2003, and Potter, 2001, as cited in Gustafson, 2005, p. 3). Furthermore, licensure requirements for new administrators have simultaneously increased in amount, in rigor, and in expense, which also reduces applicants. These demands on prospective and practicing administrators increase daily, with a negative impact on recruiting efforts. At the same time, universities and public schools alike are being asked to document their success in improving student performance in order to maintain accreditation and/or employment. These major changes have combined to create a "perfect storm" for educational leadership that requires parallel changes in both universities and public schools related to leadership preparation programs.

INEFFECTIVE PREPARATION PROGRAMS

Educational leaders trained in traditional leadership preparation programs have often indicated that their university preparation programs did not prepare them for the world they faced upon entry into the administrative world:

> Most said their training programs did not touch on the more complex combinations of leadership skills used in cultural, strategic, or external development leadership. (Portin, Schneider, DeArmond, & Gundlach, 2003, p. 38)

> I don't think that universities ever prepared me. (Ivory & Acker-Hocevar, 2005, p. 5)

Furthermore, many new principals have indicated that they learned more from their first-year experiences on the job than from their preparation programs:

> Regardless of their training, most principals think they learned the skills they need "on the job." (Portin et al., 2003, p. 37)

This disconnect between the ivory-tower idealism and the grim realities faced by educational leaders today is rapidly escalating and is exacerbated by the sanctions of NCLB and accreditation institutions (National Council for Accreditation of Teacher Education [NCATE], North Central Association [NCA], etc.). These difficulties must be addressed now if universities and schools are to be viable institutions of leadership training and learning in today's world of education.

Graduates of leadership preparation programs are not the only ones who describe these programs as ineffective and inappropriate. Following a long-term comprehensive study of administrator preparation programs in 2005, Arthur Levine, of Columbia University, found that the majority of existing administrator preparation programs were unsuccessful in preparing school leaders:

> This study found the overall quality of educational administration programs in the United States to be poor. The majority of programs range from inadequate to appalling, even at some of the country's leading universities. (Levine, 2005, p. 23)

Levine (2005) listed several reasons that explain why such programs were unsuccessful, and he identified a nine-point template for judging the quality of school leadership programs: purpose, curricular coherence, curricular balance, faculty composition, admissions, degrees, research, finances, and assessment (pp. 12–13).

Coincidentally, as public schools began coping with escalating expectations for documenting student proficiency in reading and math, university programs preparing educational leaders were being criticized for being ineffective. Some programs were unable to demonstrate any effect at all on building leadership skills:

> Specifically, we know very little about issues ranging from how we recruit and select students, instruct them in our programs, and monitor and assess their progress. . . . In particular, there is almost no empirical evidence on the education of those who educate prospective school leaders. (Murphy & Vriesenga, 2004, p. 28)

INCREASING CHALLENGES FACING PUBLIC SCHOOLS AND UNIVERSITIES

As universities struggle with the challenges of preparing effective leaders, school administrators struggle with expectations for success with every child in their schools and districts, no matter what student needs might exist. As all schools face the sanctions-based evaluation system, NCLB, school leaders must become knowledgeable about ways to help every underperforming student and group achieve the required proficiency scores in the areas of reading and math. School leaders are anxiously working to make difficult adjustments to a flawed, hierarchical system of schooling that was designed when it was acceptable to ensure that most students were successful. Principals understand that to retain their positions, their schools must meet the requirements of NCLB.

Universities also face new pressures to provide performance assessment information for their preparation programs. The program review process for NCATE now requires the submission of multiple assessments that provide evidence of candidate mastery of specialized professional association standards (NCATE, 2004). In response to these requirements, universities are in the process of developing innovative and flexible programs within traditional systems.

EMERGING RESEARCH

There is hope for a solution to these problems. Research does exist to guide us in developing and improving partnerships for preparing highly qualified educational leaders. Over the past several years, the findings of a number of large research projects have clearly indicated that uniting schools and universities is a better way to prepare administrative leaders, with a background in research-based practices applied to real-world scenarios. For example, 16 states of the Southern Regional Education Board (SREB) identified six strategies from research and from direct experiences with schools, universities, and state agencies that could be and should be used to develop highly qualified principals: "Single out high performers; recalibrate preparation programs; emphasize real-world training, link principal licensure to performance; move accomplished teachers into school leadership positions, and use state academies to cultivate leadership teams in middle-tier schools" (Bottoms, O'Neill, Fry, & Hill, 2003, pp. 2–3). SREB has now established a network of 11 universities that have redesigned leadership preparation and development programs using these strategies and continue to collect data from these nontraditional administrative preparation programs.

More recently, a meta-analysis of more than 5,000 studies and 2,894 schools and approximately 14,000 teachers, 1.1 million students, and 652 principals was completed by McREL (Waters, Marzano, & McNulty, 2003). From these studies, specific leadership responsibilities and practices were identified that are significantly correlated with student achievement. These responsibilities were cross-checked with the *ISLLC Standards for School Leaders* (1996), a guiding framework for administrative licensure in several states. The follow-up study by McREL, *The Leadership We Need* (Waters & Grubb, 2004), identified changes needed for administrator preparation. Researchers' recommendations included the development of programs to teach the knowledge and skills needed for principals to be able to use research-based leadership skills, hiring teachers who have a deep understanding of those research-based practices, and collaboration of all school officials to support second-order change (Waters & Grubb, 2004).

Clearly, universities and school districts have mutual needs that could be met by pooling talents, resources, and expertise. University and school collaborative partnerships can provide mutually beneficial solutions to the vexing problems facing both institutions. Universities provide research-based best practices and theoretical frameworks for improving student performance. Schools provide real-world settings for application, analysis, evaluation, and monitoring of practices to improve student performance. A dynamic model that pulls theory and practice together into a revolving, long-term relationship can develop around a new vision of leadership with a strong theoretical basis, and ongoing practice can strengthen both institutions. The curriculum can be collaboratively developed in an integrated, spiraling fashion, provided in field-based settings and based on strong, research-based standards. Students, professors, and administrators can learn to lead together, each playing reciprocal roles as leaders, followers, teachers, and learners. Collaborative university and school partnerships that face up to the stark realities facing both institutions can develop strong, student-centered solutions that result in simultaneous, continuous growth and revitalization of both organizations and those working in them.

PARTNERSHIPS ADDRESS THE OBSTACLES

The time is ripe for university preparation programs to join forces with practitioners to find solutions to current educational dilemmas—solutions that are mutually beneficial and will develop quality leaders at all levels of both organizations, exemplary leaders capable of thriving on the challenges they will face. But this will not be easily accomplished, and many obstacles will be encountered.

First, not everyone in universities or in school settings is open to changing past practice. However, we found in our experiences that this was not the obstacle we had anticipated: There are many educators in each of the four critical player roles who are interested and willing to get involved. The conversations can begin with those available. Second, there will always be limits imposed by inadequate available resources, governance structures, and regulatory standards. Those committed to improving leadership will work through obstacles by directing conversations toward what *can* be done, rather than wasting energies lamenting what is not possible. Indeed, changes in structural limitations can occur if a strong case is made for other options. To get around fiscal limitations, we have worked with groups of school districts joining forces on a single partnership project to share costs.

Not all school districts are located geographically near potential university partners. With the technology options available today, this barrier should be quickly set aside. Possible options here are limited only by the willingness of partners to change traditional communication practices. We have partnered with single districts located in our own immediate area, and we have also worked with two to three school districts forming joint partnerships, even though the districts were separated by up to four or five hours of driving time. It is easy to imagine partners from several hours away who are able to establish workable partnering arrangements through technology. Another model we are just beginning to explore involves single or a small number of participants coming from a sizable number of very small districts and joining together online. Working out partnership terms that meet the diverse needs of many different partners is another challenge, but not an insurmountable obstacle that will limit conversations with those interested. We are also encountering increasing interest in partnership formats that focus on building leadership capacity in teachers who intend to remain in classroom assignments—yet another dimension of leadership that can also be addressed by combining the talents and expertise of the four critical players in our scenarios.

SUMMARY

We challenge educators in leadership positions (university instructors, superintendents, principals, and leaders-in-training) to join us in finding ways to upgrade, improve, and revitalize educational leadership programs in their own settings. We have found university and public school collaborative partnerships to be an effective way to prepare successful, caring leaders for schools.

2

Using Successful Leadership Practice to Inform Theory

I don't think that universities ever prepared me. I think that what prepared me is all the different jobs I had.

—G. Ivory & M. Acker-Hocevar (2005)

Until recently, leadership scholars seldom directed their efforts toward the field of education. However, today an unprecedented amount of attention is being directed to leadership in education—we know what it looks like and why it is important. This is the good news from the research. The bad news is how poorly many institutions are preparing leaders for the educational environment that currently exists in real schools. There are certain leadership behaviors particularly related to such success.

Material from Ivory, G., & Acker-Hocevar, M. (2005). *Voices from the Field: Phase 3.* Superintendent focus group interview transcripts. Texas: University Council for Educational Administration. Used with permission.

Material from Gustafson, D. M. (2005). *A Case Study of a Professional Administrative Leadership Academy.* Unpublished doctoral dissertation, Kansas State University, Manhattan. Used with permission.

Furthermore, we must do a better job of aligning preparation programs with current practice.

The new vision for preparing leaders will include all four critical partners introduced in the previous chapter: professors, chief school administrators, building administrators, and educational leaders-in-training. To accurately reflect the conditions leaders face in real schools, all these players must be represented in the design of improved preparation programs. Practices of successful leaders will inform theory and strengthen leadership development programs.

This chapter clarifies elements of successful leadership in school today and demonstrates the shared responsibility for learning at all levels within the system.

WHO IS RESPONSIBLE FOR STUDENT LEARNING?

The central theme of this book is this: We are ALL responsible for preparing leaders who can not only survive, but thrive on the new realities that face educators, as illustrated by the following dialogue:

> "Who here is responsible for student learning?"
>
> "I am," the professors will state.
> "I am," the superintendents will respond.
> "I am," the principals will tell you.
> "I am," the leaders-in-training will say.
>
> "Who is responsible for student learning?"
>
> Answer: *"Everyone."*

SOURCE: Adapted from Conzemius & O'Neill, 2001, p. 1.

Many leadership functions can be performed at any level of the organization. For example, one identified leadership responsibility is *stimulating people to think differently about their work* (Marzano, Waters, & McNulty, 2005). Individuals in positions throughout the system can practice this with coworkers. On the other hand, some functions are better carried out at one particular level or by members of a leadership team. For example, leaders in formal positions of authority should retain responsibility for building a shared vision for the organization (Leithwood, Aitken, & Jantzi, 2006).

The terms *distributed leadership* and *building leadership capacity* are used by other researchers who also affirm the importance of leadership at all levels (Elmore, 2000; Lambert, 2003; Spillane, 2006). This important vision of shared leadership at all levels is a message for those who design programs for preparing educational leaders, and it is also important to those who want to support the professional growth of practicing leaders.

Teaching the leader behaviors that encourage leadership at all levels and recognize the barriers to building leadership capacity is critical for success of preparation programs. The perceived leaders (professors, superintendents, principals) cannot do it all—but they are responsible for seeing that it all gets done. School leaders need to be trained to develop leadership teams that allow them to do some of the leadership responsibilities and share other responsibilities to members of their leadership teams (Marzano et al., 2005). Leaders-in-training also have an important role to play as these programs develop. Students have important ideas about what they want from their leadership programs. Emerging research on distributed leadership is most comforting to these leaders-in-training as they learn about all the responsibilities today and that they are not expected to be the lone leader.

Leadership is a relationship of social influence. School leadership does not begin and end with the principal, although that position is vital. From a distributed perspective on leadership, Spillane (2006) identified three essential elements: practice, interactions, and the situation. The *practice* of leadership focuses on how leaders do what they do—how leaders set tasks in the day-to-day work of schools that encourage teachers to work collaboratively. *Interactions* of leadership and followers and their situations generate the practice leaders put to use in the workplace. The *situation* brings definition to the leadership practice and is at the same time itself defined by leadership practice: The way we react to the situation defines the situation. Leaders build leadership capacity throughout the system by giving others the chance to practice leadership, to interact with others in solving problems effectively, and to learn from the situations faced at all levels within the system.

The importance of leadership at all levels can be based on three basic truths (Reeves, 2006): Employees in any organization are volunteers; leaders have authority to make decisions but can implement them only through collaboration; and leverage happens through networks, not individuals. Our experiences with nontraditional university and school partnerships have demonstrated to us and our partners that working together, joining all the key partners collaboratively, results in a much stronger, growth-oriented leadership preparation program that demonstrates how leaders-in-training can lead from wherever they are in the organization.

THE NEW REALITIES

Public education is noted for its resistance to changing current practice and for the less than lightning speed at which any change occurs. When the call for school reform began building in the 1970s, the stagnant design of public schools was illustrated by an oft-used anecdote about Rip Van Winkle awakening from a long sleep. The only thing he recognized from his former environment was the school—which appeared unchanged from his day. There are few other institutions in our culture today that could be similarly portrayed.

Most likely, anyone whose routines connect to education today would quickly point out to an awakening Rip Van Winkle that pupils in the classroom are very different from those of his day. Teachers would tell him the students of the new millennium are very different even from those of the preceding decades. They might tell Mr. Van Winkle that if he sticks around awhile, he would observe even more profound differences in the parents of today's students! Certainly, both groups are far removed from the images of the agrarian setting Mr. Van Winkle would have known. The radical differences that exist today in all aspects of schooling absolutely change the vision needed for preparing current and future leaders for these schools and communities.

Peter Drucker (1989) predicted long ago that in the coming years, education would change more than it had "since the modern school was created by the printed book over three hundred years ago" (p. 232). Drucker also predicted that education would have a social purpose and that educators should not establish barriers between those who were highly schooled and those who were not. He foresaw that for the first time ever, schools would be expected to educate all of the children, of all of the people, all of the time. No Child Left Behind of 2001 (NCLB) formalized this expectation in a tightly structured framework of accountability, but some schools were already on that path.

Much has been written about the changing face of educational leadership, and educators can peruse a growing body of research from various credible sources. Practicing administrators often stress the changes when asked to share their ideas in personal interviews and forums. The demands today make it very clear that the days of the Lone Ranger or Superwoman leaders are over. Principals or superintendents who see the job as providing a shield from any problem, and as protecting the organization from conflict and distress, will not last long. This fantasy of leading alone must be replaced with the recognition that the leader's role today is to bring the right people together with the available resources, find the best resolution possible at the time, and be able to use the information at hand. The charismatic leader who was idolized in the past has not proven very effective in implementing lasting education reform. And, unfortunately, many promising reform initiatives are too often abandoned when such leaders move on.

Today's leaders need a new and different set of skills in their toolboxes. Today's leaders need to know *how* and *when* to use *which skills* most effectively, and preparation program planners need to include these new realities by combining their knowledge and experiences with the research about what successful leaders do. Leaders-in-training need to know what it looks like when leaders' actions make a positive difference for stakeholders. These prospective leaders want to know what it looks like inside schools when successful leaders perform their work. As an example of this need, Gustafson (2005) quoted an educational leader-in-training expressing personal expectations for a preparation program:

> I am hoping to gain more real life pictures of how to be a principal than just the textbook application. I want to know, how would one go out and do this. (p. 104)

SUCCESSFUL LEADERS MAKE A POSITIVE DIFFERENCE IN STUDENT ACHIEVEMENT

There has never been a more important time to study leadership, given the present emphasis on accountability for school and student performance. Research confirms what good teachers and administrators have known for a long time: Leadership does influence student learning. Successful leaders focus on learning and make a positive difference on student achievement. A wealth of emerging research now exists to document the positive impact of successful leadership on student performance (Interstate School Leaders Licensure Consortium [ISLLC], 1996; Waters, Marzano, & McNulty, 2003).

Leadership, teaching, and adult actions matter, and particular leadership actions are linked to improved student achievement and educational equity (Reeves, 2006). Leadership has been identified as second only to classroom instruction among all school-related factors contributing to what a student learns at school (Leithwood, Louis, Anderson, & Wahlstrom, 2004). Therefore preparation programs and planners of those programs must have an understanding of this important connection between leadership and student achievement and be able to share that information effectively with leaders-in-training.

In addition to the strong relationship between leadership and student achievement, the study by Waters et al. (2003) identified 21 leadership responsibilities that correlate with student achievement. Those who prepare leaders for our schools must know how leaders apply those responsibilities and what it looks like when successful leaders practice those responsibilities. This ability takes on even greater importance in light of another finding in the same study that leadership can have a *positive* impact on achievement or it can have a *marginal* or a *negative* impact on achievement. Leaders in today's schools must know how to be a positive influence on student achievement, know how to be in that high range as often as possible, and know which practices could lead to a negative impact. Today's educational leaders "must be the force that creates collaboration and cohesion around school learning goals and the commitment to achieve those goals" (National Association of Elementary School Principals [NAESP], 2001, p. 1).

Learning-focused leaders must emphasize curriculum, instruction, and learning. They must be able to work with teachers and others to carry out the processes related to developing the abilities of each member of the organization and be able to contribute positively to the results identified for students. They must guide others in deciding what data to collect, how to organize that information, and how to make use of the findings to guide future decisions. Learning-focused leaders understand the importance of appropriate uses of technologies to support learning and managing processes leading to those goals.

Successful leaders know that results are important, but they also realize the difference between short- and long-term goals. Long before the discussions concerning the accountability measures in NCLB, Drucker (1989) wrote that the true assessment of school would be to test graduates 10 years later. The best measure of all our efforts in schools is whether today's students become the people we would want to live by and work with in the future. In other words, programs for preparing leaders should be judged by the success of their students *after* they finish the programs, much as schools should be judged by the success of their graduates after they graduate.

SUCCESSFUL LEADERS CARRY OUT SIMPLE, BASIC PRACTICES

An increasing number of researchers are focusing their studies explicitly on basic practices of successful leaders in education. Three sets of simple practices make up the basic core of what successful leaders do: setting directions, developing people, and developing the organization (Leithwood et al., 2006). Leadership can be learned and—with further study—can be improved. In the scenarios of Chapter 1, believing that leadership could be learned is what prompted Superintendent DeBoyce and Principal Yarley to seek assistance from Professor Scatain, but it also contributed to the frustrations expressed by leader-in-training Weiss as he struggled to find meaning in his preparation program.

Setting directions has the greatest influence on the effectiveness of leadership and involves building a shared vision, setting group goals, and encouraging high performance from all. Practices in this category include giving staff an overall purpose for their work; helping staff develop consensus around district and school priorities, connecting decisions to group goals; and encouraging staff to be effective innovators (Leithwood et al., 2006).

Developing people means providing individualized support, intellectual stimulation, and an appropriate model for others. Examples of such practices are finding resources for professional development of staff, recognizing staff as individuals and respecting their unique needs, leading as much by doing as by telling, being willing to change practice as a result of what has been learned, and serving as a model for success and accomplishment within the profession (Leithwood et al., 2006).

The third set of practices, *developing the organization,* involves creating a collaborative culture, restructuring the organization, and building positive relationships with families and communities. Leaders accomplish this by promoting a climate of caring and trust, involving the staff in decisions, establishing working conditions that facilitate collaboration for planning and professional growth, distributing leadership broadly with respect for diversity of opinion, and incorporating community characteristics and values in the school (Leithwood et al., 2006).

These three sets of practices are consistent with findings from earlier leadership studies, including those from the business field, and provide an organizing tool leaders can use to help sort through the many decisions they face. Successful leaders know what not to do, and they affirm what Drucker observed in 1991, that there is nothing more wasteful than doing efficiently what need not be done at all. The downfall of low-performing schools is often not lack of effort or motivation, but making poor decisions regarding *what* to work on (Marzano et al., 2005). The *right* work includes implementing strategies that have the greatest chance of making the positive difference in student performance that the school seeks. The right work also includes recognizing challenges of the future by adding technology, diversity, and developing relationships to the curriculum.

Sometimes, leaders must make decisions about abandoning certain activities as priorities change, and stakeholders may not be good at letting go of comfortable behaviors. Successful school leaders must sometimes introduce uncomfortable conversations by, for example, asking teachers to abandon a favorite classroom unit or cancel a popular field trip that is unrelated to goals for students. Sometimes, the conversations are about setting priorities for time, such as discontinuing the practice of spending student class time on a charity project sponsored by a major business partner in the community. Leaders must make tough decisions about the right work—work that is worthy of the time and human resources required in light of the contribution made to long-term goals for students. As they face impending decisions, leaders may find it helpful to take into consideration where such decisions might fall in Leithwood's categories.

Leading has been described as a process of influencing others to achieve mutually agreed-upon purposes for the organization (Patterson, 1993). This influence implies relationships among people, which aligns nicely with "developing the people," mentioned previously. These relationships were also described by Lambert (2003)—contributing to, learning from, and influencing the learning of others and creating the opportunities for others to learn.

Successful schools require continual learning, and leaders should remain focused on both instructional and managerial tasks, mentioned by Leithwood as "designing the organization." The NAESP (2001) described principal leaders as "Those Who Care About Creating and Supporting Quality in Schools." The principal who successfully balances instructional and managerial tasks will (1) create and foster a community of learners, (2) embody learner-centered leadership, (3) seek leadership contributions from multiple sources, and (4) tie the daily operations of the schoolhouse to school and student learning goals (NAESP, 2001, pp. 10–13).

The inclusion of *managing* in the vision of the new leader is important to note. Earlier visions of leadership often stressed differences between managing and leading, indicating that each was exclusive of the other. In fact, successful administrators cannot ignore the tasks of managing daily operations—creating systems of workable routines and engaging others, as appropriate, in making schools run effectively. Successful leaders recognize the importance of managing areas such as hiring, budgeting, and scheduling. Effective management allows resources, including staff energies, to be concentrated on the mission and goals, including improvement efforts, without distractions or waste. Wise leaders also know that successful organizations require stability and that in order to be instructional leaders, the infrastructure that allows such leadership must be managed carefully.

SUCCESSFUL LEADERS LEAD PROFESSIONAL LEARNING COMMUNITIES

No architect ever built a temple alone. (Reeves, 2006, p. 28)

Likewise, no single person can achieve the essential demands of leadership alone. Because no single leader can possess every dimension of effective leaders, Reeves introduced the term *complementary leadership* and described the challenge of educational organizations to create an environment in which leaders are empowered to create complementary teams.

The key to improving school leadership begins with demystifying it. High-leverage routines and procedures must be clarified in order to develop exemplary leaders from average human beings. Leadership should be redefined around *professional learning communities*: team-based, cooperative arrangements between instructors and administrators. New fundamentals can be viewed as simple, core practices, and the goal of leadership becomes self-managed teams (Schmoker, 2005).

Good leadership in schools is shifting rapidly from a vision of a single individual as leader to one of a *leadership team.* A leadership team can address all responsibilities of leaders; single individuals cannot. The successful leader in education today nurtures the development of high-performing, effective teams that do the right work. Many researchers now refer to these teams as *professional learning communities* (or PLCs), and a growing body of professional literature on the topic currently exists.

The work of these researchers is consistent with what is happening as schools refine their efforts to improve student performance. Many school leaders are already working to develop PLCs. The NAESP (2001) described these communities as places where all stakeholders are responsible for their own learning and that of others; behind this definition is the belief that "when adults stop learning, so do students" (p. 10). Those involved in preparing leaders need to also be responsible for their own learning. And leaders-in-training must develop the skills they will need to manage their own ongoing professional growth as they facilitate the learning of others.

Leading learning communities is the responsibility of all stakeholders. NAESP has identified six standards and developed assessment rubrics. The NAESP (2001) guide provides these suggestions for those who would lead PLCs.

Standard 1: Balance Management and Leadership Roles

Effective principals lead schools in a way that places student and adult learning at the center.

Standard 2: Set High Expectations and Standards

Effective principals set high expectations and standards for the academic and social development of all students and the performance of adults.

Standard 3: Demand Content and Instruction That Ensure Student Achievement

Effective principals demand content and instruction that ensure student achievement of agreed-upon academic standards.

Standard 4: Create a Culture of Adult Learning

Effective principals create a culture of continuous learning for adults that is tied to student learning and other school goals.

Standard 5: Use Multiple Sources of Data as Diagnostic Tools

Effective principals use multiple sources of data as diagnostic tools to assess, identify, and apply instructional improvement.

Standard 6: Actively Engage the Community

Effective principals actively engage the community to create shared responsibility for student and school success.

SOURCE: NAESP (2001, pp. 6–7).

In practice, many schools are forming PLC teams that meet on a designated schedule to focus on student learning. Ensuring that all students learn is the main purpose of these groups. Following the pattern suggested in DuFour, Eaker, and DuFour's (2005) work, these groups use a framework of three questions:

1. What do we want students to learn?
2. How will we know if they learn it?
3. What will we do if a student does not learn it?

Some add a fourth question to address the needs of highly able learners:

4. What will we do if they already know it?

Leaders can create a culture through PLCs that develop ways of doing all business throughout the school community, not just events on the schedule. In fact, the preparation program partnership, by involving university and district professionals and leaders-in-training, also becomes a PLC and provides strong modeling of lifelong learning for the leaders-in-training.

LEADERS DEVELOP LEADERSHIP THROUGHOUT THE SYSTEM

Those who would successfully lead school improvement must believe that everyone has the capacity for working as a leader and accept responsibility for building capacity in others to make that happen. Principals should be judged as successful, not on the basis of programs put in place, but on the basis of how many new leaders are emerging around them. There is little chance that large-scale reform will happen without an emphasis on capacity building throughout the system at all levels (Fullan, 2005). The focus for all stakeholders should be on building leadership capacity in themselves and those around them in the community. Change is already under way in valuing the importance of teacher, parent, and student leadership, and these changes are evident in our redesigned vision of leadership.

OTHER ESSENTIAL PRACTICES

Successful leaders periodically step out for the "balcony view" (Heifetz & Linsky, 2002, as cited in Fullan, 2005, p. 103) to assess the progress the overall system is making toward the results. Time, energy, and fiscal resources are always in limited supply. Successful leaders choose how available resources can best support student success—this includes the energy of human resources and the time available to dedicate to the work of the system. Leaders must know *what* to do, *how* to do it, and *when* to do it, as revealed by Waters et al.'s (2003) leadership framework research. Whatever terms we use to describe leadership are far less important than, first, knowing what a good leader *does* that makes a difference in student outcomes and, second, teaching leaders-in-training to recognize those practices.

Other researchers look closely at what successful education leaders do on the job. Implementation, execution, and monitoring are more important than planning and process when it comes to achievement and equity. The effective leader knows the importance of working in the following dimensions of leadership, identified by Reeves (2006).

1. *Visionary Leadership.* Articulating a common vision and clearly linking actions for accomplishing it.
2. *Relational Leadership.* Skills that account for nearly three times the impact as analytical skills have on the system.
3. *Systems Leadership.* Recognizing the complexity and simplicity of the organization.
4. *Reflective Leadership.* Bridging the gap between theory abstractions and daily lives.
5. *Collaborative Leadership.* Balancing individual discretion, collaborative decisions, and unilateral leadership decisions.
6. *Analytical Leadership.* Seeking to be a master of persistent questions, rather than of answers.
7. *Communicative Leadership.* The ability to articulate ideas.

SOURCE: Terms from Reeves (2006, pp. 32–60); definitions paraphrased by authors.

A principal's presence can positively influence student performance by adding these components: awareness (seeing firsthand where the action is in the school); visibility (the principal's visible presence is a statement of reassurance and familiarity, while offering a healthy dose of fear and order—monitoring and supervising); clarity (the principal has more information that can be useful in clarifying thinking); and relationships (the principal builds them with all participants in the school community) (Hall, 2005).

Another dimension of leadership was added by DuFour et al. (2005) that warned against being too focused on teaching and not enough on learning. Leaders must know about assessment—what is good design and how to analyze data produced about student learning. If leaders-in-training are to develop the skills to both understand and implement these dimensions, a strong blend of theory and field experience will be required.

Others place much emphasis on teaming. Research by Marzano et al. (2005) concluded that leadership starts with a radical commitment to a guaranteed and viable curriculum. It is the role of the leader to bring that about and monitor its effectiveness. However, it is unrealistic to assume that the leader can make this happen alone. Two important components of successful leadership in our new vision are the ability to develop PLCs and the ability to build leadership capacity throughout the system.

WHAT TEACHERS THINK ABOUT LEADERSHIP

Stressing the importance of leadership and studying its effects on student achievement doesn't take away any of the importance of the quality of the teacher and of what happens in the classroom. It does tell us that good teachers accomplish the most when supported by quality leadership, and it provides great cause for us to focus on what leaders *do* that makes a difference.

Those that believe teacher attitude is a factor influencing student performance will see another connection between leadership and student performance. Teachers themselves believe that leadership is an important influence on student performance. In 2006, the Center for Teaching Quality, an organization in Chapel Hill, North Carolina, that promotes teacher leadership, partnered with the Kansas National Education Association, the Kansas United School Administrators, and the governor of Kansas to survey approximately 22,000 Kansas teachers and administrators concerning working conditions in Kansas schools related to five areas: time during the work day, school facilities and resources, school leadership, teacher empowerment, and professional development. Teachers from virtually every Kansas district participated in the 53% response rate. Results (Kansas Teachers Working Conditions Survey, 2006) included the following items of interest:

- 36% selected school leadership as the one aspect of the work environment most affecting the willingness to "keep teaching at your school."
- 14% selected school leadership as the aspect most important in promoting student learning.
- 97% ranked support from school leadership as "important" to "extremely important" in influencing their decisions about future plans.
- 59% of respondents "agreed" or "strongly agreed" that school leadership in their buildings is effective.

SUMMARY

Research on educational leadership reveals elements of successful practice that must be included in preparation programs for future school leaders. Leaders build capacity in others and form strong teams that replace the vision of the "superhero leader" of the past. Strong leaders are not threatened by leadership emerging throughout the system; they realize success depends on it. The four critical players introduced in Chapter 1 (universities, district leaders, building leaders, and leaders-in-training) are recognizing the responsibility they share for developing successful leadership programs and practices. Superintendent DeBoyce wants to develop leadership throughout the system. Principal Yarley needs to know how to lead the PLCs that will make her school successful. Professor Scatain wants all of the administrators he prepares to be able to make a positive difference in student achievement. Leader-in-training Weiss wants to learn what successful leaders do, on his way to becoming a successful school leader. By combining efforts, calling on both theory and best practice, and appreciating the value each contributes to the task, the four can successfully address their concerns.

3

Using Leadership Theory to Inform Practice

When we choose who will lead us, we are also choosing where we wish to be led.

—Anonymous

Establishing a new vision for educational leadership based on practice should not cause us to ignore what can be learned about leadership theory from other sources. A basic premise of this book is that strong educational leaders can be developed using a three-stage process of knowledge and theory acquisition, guided practice, and individual and group reflection. When theory and practice are firmly connected, these three stages occur concurrently with university faculty, leaders-in-training, and exemplary educational leaders moving back and forth between the role of mentor and that of mentee. Involving individuals in discussions about leadership theories and styles allows them to gain skills and knowledge about the various strengths and weaknesses of various forms of leadership. This process also allows the participants to identify their own strengths and weaknesses as leaders.

At the same time they are gaining the theoretical grounding for effective leadership, participants are also involved in guided leadership experiences. Concurrent with knowledge acquisition and clinical application, they are engaged in individual and group reflection on the leadership process. By mastering knowledge about leadership and incorporating skill sets into their own leadership styles, these individuals become more able to lead. Although leading by knowledge alone is similar to managing, leading without knowledge is irresponsible.

Leadership has been defined as "an influence relationship among leaders and followers who intend real changes that reflect their mutual purposes" (Rost, 1991, p. 102). Implicit in this definition is the belief that leadership is a process, not a position. Successful change is the result of systemwide collaboration, rather than the actions of an individual. However, any change requires a leader who mobilizes the organization, community group, nation, or society to improve. Therefore to prepare leaders, we must first believe that leadership can be learned. Teaching leadership requires knowledge of the multiple dimensions that, when applied, can produce a result that is more than the sum of its parts.

LEADERSHIP CAN BE LEARNED

There are some who think that leaders are men or women who were born with an extraordinary ability to lead. Others say that leadership is accidental or situational; they say that the circumstances make the leader. It has also been said that most people will never be leaders. We challenge all three of these assumptions. This book describes a process that demonstrates that leadership can be taught and it can be learned. As the study of leadership has become more popular, scholars have categorized leadership into the following three broad categories: transactional, transformational, and transforming.

Transactional leadership is based on the assumption that people are motivated primarily by reward and punishment. Consequently, such leaders believe that society will function more efficiently with a clear chain of command. Members of society will negotiate work for reward. Managers make decisions. Transactional leaders work in a clear structure, where rewards and punishments keep order. In the leadership-versus-management continuum, transactional leadership is very much toward the management end of the scale. The transactional educational leader would say, "You are hired as a teacher, the school district pays you, and you will do the work I assign you." Transactional educational leaders maintain the status quo, focusing on managing the daily operation of the school and believing that change, if it occurs at all, should be slow.

This type of leader might be described as *doing things right* rather than being concerned with *doing the right thing*. Transactional leaders are often referred to as "bureaucratic leaders." They strongly believe in rules and the rights of those in authority. Their main mode of operation is bargaining and negotiation for resources and power. Transactional leaders expect obedience based on their positions and the agreement to accept obligations and commands. Generally, advancement is based on seniority or achievement and is dependent on judgment of superiors. However, allegiance is owed not to a person, but to his or her position in the bureaucracy. This type of leader has the advantage of efficiency. However, the primary disadvantage is that most power resides at the top of the hierarchy and so their followers generally have a sense of powerlessness.

In contrast, *transformational leaders* are concerned with not only *what* is done but also *how* things are done, and they seek to satisfy the higher needs of their followers (Burns, 1978). These leaders seek to engage the follower as a full person. Leaders of this type consciously seek and embrace change. They are interested in improving the organization and the lives of the people served. Transformational leaders believe that if their followers believe in the importance of the objective, they will be highly motivated to focus on the task and produce better work.

Transformational leadership can be defined in terms of how the leader affects his or her followers, who are intended to trust, admire, and respect their leader. The transformational leader transforms followers by increasing their awareness of task importance and value; by getting them to focus first on team or organizational goals, rather than their own interests; and by stimulating their higher-order needs. Transformational leaders use charisma to induce strong emotions and to cause their followers to identify with them. These leaders depend on emotional appeals, coaching, and mentoring to motivate their followers (Bass, 1990a).

Transforming leadership is the third type of leadership and is the ultimate goal for educational leaders. Transforming leaders are interested in changing a person's heart (Burns, 1978). An example of such leadership can be seen in President John Kennedy's (1961) call to "ask not what your country can do for you—ask what you can do for your country." The transforming leader is interested in the philosophical assumptions of the status quo. While both transformational and transforming leaders are concerned about justice and the common good of society, the transforming leader is concerned with raising the essential moral nature of leadership. Transforming leaders want to alter the basic value system of society. For them, evaluating cannot be done merely according to the scale of effects. Evaluation must also embody the aspirations of a people for liberty, equality, and the pursuit of happiness (Burns, 1978).

Providing a formula specifying which type of leadership to use, and when, is difficult, but transforming leaders exhibit traits from all three styles of leadership, choosing styles that fit the situation, organizational goals, and their own beliefs.

THE DIMENSIONS OF LEADERSHIP

In preparation for this publication, we searched "leadership books" on Amazon.com and found 50,541 references. Clearly, there is no shortage of people telling us what leaders need to know. Consequently, the following section is not an effort to provide a comprehensive catalog of requisite leadership knowledge. It is, rather, an introductory discussion of critical dimensions of leadership that should be part of the basic framework of any educational leadership preparation program:

- Context for change
- Creating a vision
- Communicating a vision
- Strategic planning and goal setting
- Personnel issues
- Empowerment
- Making decisions and taking risks
- Leadership with honor
- Coping with stress

Context for Change

Whether referred to as visionary, charismatic, transformational, inspirational, or postheroic leadership, there is a new generation of leadership theory (Bass, 1985; Bennis & Nanus, 1985). Whereas past theories were based on scientific management and psychological behaviorism, this new generation of leadership is described in terms of vision, empowerment, social responsibility, and transformation. New leaders should be able to invent and create institutions that can empower employees to satisfy their needs, with the end result of empowerment and an organizational culture that helps employees generate a sense of meaning in their work and a desire to challenge themselves to experience success (Bennis & Nanus, 1985). Others suggest that leadership may emerge as the most needed element, in the highest demand and shortest supply (Peters, 1987). New leaders should be able to move followers to higher degrees of consciousness, such as liberty, freedom, justice, and self-actualization.

When discussing transformational leadership, many writers use *charisma* to describe the leader. The word is derived from the Greek and literally means "divine favor." The concept has been known since biblical times and refers to the ability to prophesize, rule, teach, convey wisdom, and heal. German sociologist and economist Max Weber (1946) formally developed the concept of charisma in relation to his conceptualization of authority. Weber used the term to refer to almost superhuman powers or qualities. Today, *charismatic, transformational,* and *visionary* are often used synonymously. Transformational leaders stand out from others in their force of powerful personal characteristics, their ability to appeal to ideological values and to expect self-sacrifice from their followers, and their intensely personal relationships with their followers.

Good leaders often come to leadership roles with many competencies and a belief that if they listen carefully and work together, they will do well (Birnbaum, 1992). However, strict organization charts are no longer useful. Environmental challenges, such as the demands of the marketplace and the evolution of technology, may require very different kinds of talents to respond to various challenges. For example, a school district may require a leader with very specific knowledge, while another district may require a leader who possesses a broad-brush overview of education. A leader must be able to move the right person into the right leadership position. Coping with rapid and often unpredictable change is one of the greatest challenges for educational leaders today. The ability of school districts to respond to change will be directly related to how well the educational leaders develop responsive educational leadership teams.

Creating a Vision

Leaders see things differently. Leadership begins with a vision; and without a vision, there can be no effective leadership. King Solomon stated it succinctly: "Where there is no vision, the people perish" (Prov. 29:18, RSV). For a leader, a vision is not a dream, but a reality that has not yet come into existence. Vision is palpable to leaders. Otherwise, they would not be able to devote the long hours over many years that it takes to fulfill a vision.

Vision is the creation of a focus, the development of an agenda. The key is for the leader to ask not "What can I do?" but "What needs to be done?" A vision is something that provides a mental picture, a future orientation, or a guidepost for an organization. It describes where a school district or school building is going and how it will get there. It is a picture of the future for which people are willing to work. Vision can be used to mold meaning for those who work within an organization (Manasse, 1986). These efforts of the leader to develop shared visions lead to "bonding" with the stakeholders (Sergiovanni, 1990). These leaders often become the "vision holders" or the "keepers of the dream."

Creating a vision is not a singular event. It must be an evolutionary process that develops over time. It is a process that requires continued articulation, reflection, and reevaluation. A vision is the result of purposeful tinkering. Through dozens of small efforts, each day is an opportunity to come closer to your perceived ideal.

Every leadership guru states that outstanding leaders have a vision. Although this is true, this statement is not particularly helpful. The obvious question is "Yes, but how do you create a vision?" Many authors speak about developing a vision as if it were an almost mystical process. They seem to be saying that leaders somehow develop a vision and then bring it with them when they join an organization. Upon arrival, the leader somehow imparts his or her vision onto the members of the group and then gets people to buy into the vision and align themselves with it. However, such ideas can be quite dangerous (Heifetz, 1994). Great leaders do not come up with a vision alone. They are instead similar to conductors of orchestras, skilled at embodying the soul of the music. They may also be good at articulating the transcendent values of the organization or community, as opposed to sharing their own vision(s).

In establishing a vision, the leader must look at the situation and learn. The leader must listen to people and sort through all the priorities. The leader should learn everything about the organization, its history and culture, attitudes and beliefs, and about the larger environment, which surrounds the organization. Only then will the leader be able to develop a comprehensive picture of the organization's strengths and weaknesses. The leader must allow these contextual factors to guide the development of a vision. Only then can a vision be identified.

A vision is always about the future, but it must be grounded in the here and now. Today's leaders need "bifocal vision," the ability to take care of the needs of today and meet current obligations while also focusing on the future (Harari, 1997). Ninety percent of a leader's energy should be focused on the future, with 10% focused on the day-to-day operation of the organization. The process of establishing a vision often progresses through three stages. The leader must first identify the situation that needs to be changed. The second step is to identify the elements of change that the leader wishes to foster. The final stage of developing a vision is implementing a framework for transforming the organization. Through this process, the leader helps the organization let go of what was and begin to reach for what could and should be. In developing any theme, one moves forward, then reevaluates, and then moves forward again. Progress never ends for a kinetic and organic organization.

The primary power of leadership is the *power of persuasion.* Seldom does a leader have the authority to force people to join in a new vision. The leader must provide others in the organization with the opportunity to become part of something by choice. If change is going to take place, a significant portion of the organization must become committed to that vision. A majority of the stakeholders must join with the leader in feeling fully responsible for making the vision happen. Many leaders make the mistake of thinking they have been successful if they can get the members of their organizations to genuinely want a vision to succeed. People can want something to occur, yet the vision may still be that of the leader only. Unfortunately, in many school districts and school buildings, not all staff members are enrolled in the vision, and even fewer are committed. Many school staff members are in a state of compliance. Compliant staff members do what is expected of them, but they are not truly enrolled or committed (Senge, 1990).

One of the most important qualities of a leader is the ability to provide a clear vision of the transformed future he or she imagines. At its most basic level, vision involves the ability to identify the purpose of an organization and its priorities. What makes the concept of vision more than simple goal setting and prioritizing is a willingness to believe in the seemingly impossible and a passionate commitment to creatively closing the gap between the present reality and the desired vision. Creativity, innovative thinking, boldness, courage, and the willingness to take risks are key to creating a vision. Transformational leaders have the imagination and energy to formulate a vision and are able to articulate it and facilitate its installation in others until it permeates the organization.

Leaders can talk about vision, but it is how they spend their time that reveals to other members of the organization what their core values are and what they truly believe is important. Leaders must behave in ways that model their values. By being visible, leaders accomplish the dual purpose of demonstrating what is important to them, while at the same time learning what is important to the organization at large. The transformational leader must be part of the organization, not separate from it. The transformational leader must be totally involved in the operation of the organization. Strong leaders cannot lead from a seated position.

Communicating a Vision

Communication skills are the essential tools of a leader, who must take a vision and put it into action. These skills make the critical difference in causing others to recognize and follow a leader. Communication is the vehicle by which people can perceive that an individual has talents to be respected and emulated. Good leaders empower others to lead in ways that make simultaneous feats possible, an outcome that is impossible without strong communication skills. Excellent leaders are people who exude positive energy and make others feel stronger by their words and their actions.

Strong interpersonal skills allow leaders to successfully convey the message of the vision to a wide array of audiences in myriad situations. Communicating the vision consists of explaining abstract concepts using specific examples. A leader merely saying he or she wants the organization to get better is not likely to enlist much support. Communication is one of the most fundamental skills in life and a prerequisite to problem solving (Covey, 1992). Communication could also be defined as a "mutual understanding." Some leaders treat communication and interaction as instrumental devices that become less important once they have learned about the organization; exemplary leaders are more likely to view them as essential and continuing components of evolving communities.

All communication should be open, direct, and positive. Every leader faces the challenge of providing frank and timely feedback, while simultaneously being perceived as open to the comments and concerns of others. Successful communication is accomplished through continual repetition of an individualized message. It is important to explain in detail the reason behind decisions and directives, if possible. Open communication not only enhances and builds relationships but also raises the probability that future decisions will be accepted even when explanations are not reasonable or feasible. By sharing the overall mission and vision, the leader inspires others to break down the larger vision and translate it into their own domains.

A leader's vision is communicated in all interactions through the integrity of the types of relationships developed. Canadian media guru and communications theorist Marshall McLuhan (2006) taught that "the medium is the message," meaning that the way we acquire information affects us as much or more than the information itself. All media can then be considered active metaphors in their power to translate experience into new forms.

Storytelling and providing visual images are also effective means of communication and leadership. Telling stories offers a way of carrying the history of the organization from generation to generation. Stories can be used for motivation, to put the present into perspective, and to inspire and give confidence. All great leaders have great stories, according to Tom Peters (2000). Storytelling was described by Howard Gardner (1995) as a key to leadership, because stories are how we remember, how we learn, and how we visualize what can be. Gardner suggested using stakeholders in the vision, because stories are "personal, passionate, and purposeful," and that leaders should develop a "where we are going" story as part of the vision (pp. 9–18). Martin Luther King Jr.'s "I Have a Dream" speech mobilized energy around the powerful image of social equality. In like manner, educational leaders must articulate stories that demonstrate the vision of the organization.

Strategic Planning and Goal Setting

Strategic planning is the process of translating broad goals into actions. The need for strategic planning can be seen in the following quote from Oliver Wendell Holmes:

> I find the great thing in this world is not so much where we stand, as in what direction we are moving: To reach the port of heaven, we must sail sometimes with the wind and sometimes against it—but we must sail, and not drift, nor lie at anchor. (Holmes, 2006)

Strategic planning is necessary precisely because we cannot forecast. Strategic planning does not deal with future decisions. Decisions exist only in the present. Strategic planning does not address what the organization should do tomorrow. It addresses what we have to do today to be ready for an uncertain tomorrow.

A key role of a transformational leader is the development of the networks, the relationships, and an organizational culture that allow the vision to be realized. This type of community building creates an environment in which all stakeholders can find meaning and motivation. When a leader lets individuals know they are valued members of the organization's community, that sense of connection both encourages them to work toward the vision and gives them an effective arena in which to do so.

Highly motivated people who believe strongly in something can do great things. Motivation should be placed above all attributes except judgment when evaluating leaders. Leaders must understand that workers are more effective if they can take pride in the product, the quality of their services rendered, or the known integrity of the organization (J. Gardner, 1990). Anything a leader can do to help workers feel proud of their organization serves a good purpose. A leader should take every opportunity to tell external audiences the organization's story. This continual recitation begins to have an impact when it is followed up with examples of outstanding individual efforts. The most gifted leaders know that financial incentives are only one motivating factor for their stakeholders. Most people respond very well to a word of praise. Praise indicates that constituents are noticed and valuable. Leaders who understand what motivates their followers are able to tap the emotions that lie below the surface and help them recommit to the vision of the organization.

Whereas emphasis on a leader's vision focuses on a desired outcome, the concept of transformational leadership encompasses the means as well as the end. A vision is based on values. For successful and sustained change to occur, those values must be attended to first and foremost throughout the process of implementing the vision. A transformational leader not only has the action orientation and tenacity to "just do it" but also emphasizes doing it the right way for the right reasons. This value-centered approach establishes the trust and credibility that are central to the leadership process. Credibility is critical for a leader or an organization to succeed in the long run. Credibility takes a long time to build, but it can be lost in an instant.

Personnel Issues

Perhaps the superintendent's most important responsibility is selecting the people who will be the building leaders. And certainly, selecting the people who will teach is one of the most critical decisions a building leader will make. But how does one know which people to select? It is critical to understand the integrity and the innermost nature of possible employees. Certainly, knowledge of subject matter is important in a teacher. However, many people are hired as teachers and leave the profession within their first few years. College grades and teaching test scores obviously are indicators of the quality of a person's work. However, it is not known how an individual will react in specific environments. Since each environment is different, staff selection always includes a dimension of chance.

Many leaders fail because they do not have the self-confidence needed to hire people with strong abilities, perhaps stronger than those of the perceived leaders. Instead, they practice "degenerative hiring," hiring people with lesser abilities than themselves. Successful leaders must know that if they hire someone with high ability and empower that person to do the job, everyone will win. However, before leaders can empower others, they have to trust those they lead. Transformational leaders must ask themselves, "How much do I trust the people who work here?" No significant empowerment can occur when the leader believes the team is untrustworthy. Leaders who are open to participation and empowerment believe in the inherent desire (and ability) of most people to contribute positively to their organizations (Wheatley, 1997).

By respecting and trusting the people who work with them, leaders can unleash startlingly high levels of productivity and creativity from members of the organization. One of the primary tasks of being a leader is to make sure that the organization knows itself. The process of having a vision, articulating the vision, and hiring good people is a continuous conversation about what the organization is and what it wants to be.

Leaders are expected to get the job done, and the best way to do this is to recruit people at all levels of the organization who have the answers. These are the people who can assist leaders in making the right decisions about dealing with an uncertain world. Ultimately, leaders will be represented by the people surrounding them. However, it takes great self-confidence to hire exceptional people. Conversely, if a leader is surrounded with people who lack talent, the leader will appear to be weak and insecure and the vision of the organization is unlikely to be fulfilled. At times, a leader may need to choose between being the smartest person in the school and having an exceptional school (Peters, 2000).

A good leader hires good people and then lets them do their jobs. Leaders should focus on teamwork and develop skills in their stakeholders for building consensus as well as problem solving through teamwork. In this way, they can instill loyalty and strengthen commitment to the institution. Leading by example is one of the best ways to demonstrate desired characteristics (Birnbaum, 1992). When leadership is shared in this way, organizations have multiple methods for sensing environmental change, checking for problems, and monitoring campus performance.

Effective leaders delegate a good many things. If they didn't, they would drown in trivia. No one person can do everything. The superintendent should be making the big decisions. Placing very talented people in key positions is the right thing to do. However, it takes a confident leader to be able to "lead the leaders." Leaders are important, but great team members form the bedrock of great organizations. Competent team members must sustain the leader's vision; they are the "glue" that holds the organization together. They synthesize the scores of people who power high-performing companies. Great leaders do not create followers; they create more leaders. It is possible that too many old-fashioned leaders measured their influence by the number of followers they could claim.

The greatest leaders look for more leaders rather than more followers. Empowering others to create their own destinies is an integral part of transforming leadership and of our leadership preparation mode. Models of this type of leadership include Martin Luther King, Jr., Mahatma Gandhi, Nelson Mandela, Eleanor Roosevelt, Margaret Thatcher, and Mother Teresa.

All great groups have great leaders with a keen eye for talent. Members do not simply solve problems; they are engaged in a process of discovery that is its own reward. Curiosity fuels every great organization. People do not want to be managed; they want to be led. They do not want to be told what to do; they want to be able to determine what needs to be done and then do it. People who succeed in forming and leading great groups are pragmatic dreamers who get things done but also have immortal longings. At the heart of every outstanding group is a dream of greatness, and it is that vision that drives the organization. Great leaders seem to incarnate the dream and become one with it. Although effective leaders make decisions, they are often willing to allow others to work as they see fit. Collaborative leaders appoint competent people and expect them to do their jobs (Bennis & Biederman, 1997).

Success is more likely to be achieved when leaders embrace a teamwork approach that includes the ability to innovate, achieve adaptability in adverse circumstances, or get an edge on productivity. Employees need skills in building consensus, problem solving through a team approach, instilling loyalty, and leading by example. When leadership is shared, an organization has multiple ways of sensing environmental change, checking for problems, and monitoring performance (Bensimon, 1991).

The effective leader works to release the talents and the energies present in others in support of shared vision. Leaders can use a process that induces a group to pursue shared objectives with shared beliefs concerning the standards of acceptable behavior that govern them (J. Gardner, 1990). Leadership, which can be taught and learned, requires everyone to take responsibility and to make a commitment beyond oneself. People create change, first, as individuals and groups and then as systems. Organizational forms take shape from how people understand and relate to one another, how information is distributed and communicated, and how identity is developed and maintained. People achieve the most when they participate completely and openly in a dynamic, shared process. The leader should rarely be seen as the best performer. Instead, the best leaders are invigorated by coordinating and supporting the efforts of others, not from doing the work themselves (Peters, 2000).

Empowerment

Everyone who writes about leadership talks about *empowerment,* yet there seem to be numerous definitions of just what empowerment actually is. According to Pastor (1996), empowerment resembles an evolution that happens when a person is in a relationship that has two aspects: personal empowerment (what individuals do for themselves) and group empowerment (when individuals work with others to gain empowerment).

Empowerment of others definitely does not mean the employees are simply let loose to do whatever it is they are supposed to do. Empowerment can be similar to an anointing and should not be done without any preparation or training for those empowered (Pastor, 1996). Empowerment is a process of integrating personal empowerment, responsibility, accountability, and shared risk taking. This is a dynamic and evolutionary process.

Hiring smart people and giving them responsibility is not enough, however, to ensure success. The leader must not only assign responsibility but also give the authority to get the job done. The real challenge of empowering individuals is to ensure they have the confidence to make interpretive judgments that entail real consequences, for which they must take responsibility. Understanding complexity, making judgments, and drawing conclusions are all elements of critical thinking and are all-important to a principled community. The ability to develop leadership in others requires a teachable point of view, a story for the organization, and a well-defined methodology for teaching and coaching. Emotional energy and edge allow winning leaders to naturally generate positive emotional energy in others with the drive to face reality and make tough decisions (Tichy, 1998).

Autonomy and empowerment are driven by communication between the leader and team. This process is continual. Of course, it takes time for all members of an organization to become involved in this empowerment process. Nonetheless, the transformational leader believes authentic involvement in the decision-making and policy-implementation process will result in more effective outcomes.

Making Decisions and Taking Risks

Leaders must have the confidence to make decisions—and the courage to risk making mistakes. They must be prepared to acknowledge their mistakes when they occur, learn from them, and move on. They must never give up on their pursuit of improving the organization they represent.

Leaders of effective organizations put a premium on action and trust people's intelligence, rather than requiring strict adherence to protocol. Decision making and risk taking often form the line that distinguishes leaders from everyone else (David Thompson, interview conducted by R. Shoop, October 27, 1999). Leaders need not be reckless, but they must have the ability to see opportunity, seize it, and move forward after weighing the potential outcomes and choosing a risk strategy. Variables are neither completely known nor completely controllable. Informed risk is the basis for the kind of trust that is placed in the hands of really good leaders—anything else is merely management of data. Although optimal decision making is desired, there comes a point when an individual has to recognize that the data are as good as they're going to get and action must be taken before it's too late.

A key to leadership is to be willing to make decisions and, from time to time, to take some risks. There are few business leaders today who have gotten ahead without taking a risk or being decisive:

- Former Chrysler CEO Lee Iacocca believes that the most important trait of a leader is decisiveness (Iacocca, 2006).
- T. Boone Pickens, the Texas business baron, said making decisions is the most important quality in a leader (Pickens, 2006).
- Willis R. Whitney, former director of the General Electric research laboratory, suggested that people often have "thousands of reasons why they cannot do what they want to" and that leaders can help them discover "one reason why they can" (Whitney, 2006).

Despite the best intentions, we sometimes fail. These failures can occur because of a change of circumstances, errors in judgment, or the choice of the wrong strategies. Sometimes failures can damage credibility. If leaders satisfactorily respond to their failures of leadership, constituents are usually willing to continue to follow. Leaders with the ability to accept and admit responsibility, apologize, and work quickly to address problems can still remain credible (Kouzes & Posner, 1993). A leader who encourages risk taking must allow for the possibility that mistakes will be made. Empowering leaders focus not on the mistake itself, but on what happens after the mistake is made. Generally, people find it redeeming when their leaders can admit mistakes and apologize.

Leadership is easy when all is well. Everyone enjoys good news. It is easier for leaders to avoid the risks and hazards that come from challenging people and tackle tough problems just by maintaining the status quo. Leadership in hard times is exceptionally difficult: Leaders often must tell people difficult news that, at least in the short term, appears to require a painful adjustment (Heifetz, 1994). These are the times that face educational leaders today. They can no longer just maintain the status quo; they must face the risks and ask their constituents to tackle tough problems.

To learn how to be a better leader, one must be able to learn from failures. Sometimes, the most difficult thing about learning from failure is to recognize failure when it occurs. Failure can be the result of one event, but most often the difference between success and failure lies in small tactical decisions. To lead, one must be able to face failure and then make the necessary midcourse corrections.

The strength of an organization is determined not only by the way leaders face their own failures but also by the way leaders respond to the mistakes of others. It is important to acknowledge that we are all human and we all make mistakes. Mistakes should be addressed in a direct manner, followed by a move forward.

All this suggests that the ability to admit mistakes and to apologize is important in principle and has some obvious practical utility—but at the same time, leaders who have to constantly engage in course correction have to spend too much energy on remedial behaviors. Really good leaders catch errors fairly early so that correction is not overly dramatic and is within the time frame in which people are still willing to forgive (Kouzes & Posner, 1993).

However, sometimes having a vision, a strong team, and a caring attitude is not enough. Sometimes, even with hard work, success is not guaranteed, especially in this time of high-stakes testing. Consequently, an excellent educational leader must be prepared for the difficulties that have resulted from the No Child Left Behind mandates. Leaders must be prepared to assist the educational team as they face setbacks yet continue to move forward. It must be acknowledged that those in leadership positions will fail sometimes. We all fail. The best leaders have fierce determination that allows them to continue despite problems.

Steve Jobs, CEO of Apple Computer, observed the following:

> When you ask creative people how they did something, they feel a little guilty because they didn't really do it, they just saw something. It seemed obvious to them after awhile. . . . They were able to connect experiences they've had and synthesize new things. And the reason they were able to do that was they've had more experiences or they have thought more about their experiences than other people. (Wolf, 1996)

People most likely to succeed are those who combine reasonable talent with the ability to keep going in the face of defeat. Optimism is a predictor of who will be successful doing extraordinarily difficult things under pressure (Bennis & Biederman, 1997).

Great leaders have an ambition marked by a greater sense of purpose and an urge to create something beyond themselves, and they often follow a predictable path of three stages. The first stage is deeply personal and begins with a fresh insight. Ambitious people prepare themselves to recognize—and then seize—the opportune moment. At the second stage, leaders must begin to act to achieve goals by weighing the risks of underachieving against those of overextending. Many leaders fail at this point because they are unable to deliver on their promises. Consequently, they lose credibility with those within the organization. The third stage is a difficult stage for some leaders. This is the stage at which the leader must disperse leadership to others in the organization. The leader may not be ready to step aside for the next generation, but he or she is consciously preparing for that transition. This is not an easy task, and many leaders never reach this stage (Champy, 2000).

Coping With Stress

"Stress-related illness" and "burnout" are increasingly being identified as a reality of educational leadership. Consequently, educational organizations must continually look for ways to keep their workforces happy, healthy, and productive. A sense of humor is a characteristic frequently associated with high-functioning leaders (Bass, 1990b) and with a leader's ability to effect change in followers (Hogan, Curphy, & Hogan, 1994). Many organizations attribute higher levels of employee commitment, cohesiveness, and performance to leaders' use of humor in their cultures (Hof, Rebello, & Burrows, 1996).

The use of humor in organizations has been associated with improving morale among workers, creating a more positive organizational culture (Clouse & Spurgeon, 1995), enhancing group cohesiveness, stimulating individual and group creativity (Csikszentmihalyi, 1996), and increasing motivation (Crawford, 1994). Humor has also been associated with higher levels of productivity. Humor, when properly used, can enhance the leadership processes, improve performance, and moderate the impact of stress on individual performance.

Transformational leaders should also strive to build confidence in followers, encouraging them to reframe the future and question the tried and true and coaching them to develop their full capabilities (Burns, 1978). Through the use of humor, leaders can signal to followers that they are able to handle tough situations or tasks. Humor can create a more amiable atmosphere at work, which can enhance creative interactions among employees and their performance.

Leaders who cannot laugh about their mistakes are doomed (Peters, 2000). Leaders make mistakes. Consequently, at times, they may look foolish. In situations where we have little or no control over our external circumstances, our only power lies in how we react to them. We can choose either laughter or despair. It is a great talent to be able to laugh at ourselves and our situations in times of stress. This ability helps release tension, regain perspective, and accept that which we cannot change. Historically, some have tended to devalue the idea of laughter at work, seeing it as a distraction. However, recent scientific research has found that managers who facilitated the highest level of employee performance used humor the most often. In fact, research data seem to indicate that laughter is an integral part of physical wellness:

> After a bout of laughter, blood pressure drops to a lower healthier level than before the laughter began. Laughter also oxygenates your blood, thereby increasing muscles and works out all your major internal systems like the cardiovascular and respiratory systems. (Granirer, 2001)

Consequently, more and more leaders are beginning to understand that incorporating humor into the workplace is a positive thing. Humor seems particularly helpful when people have difficult tasks to do and have limited resources in terms of time, money, policies, or people power.

Sometimes, leaders become so narrowly focused that they lose sight of the big picture. Humor can help them regain perspective. Humor can make people feel good. It releases tension, creates a sense of acceptance, conveys a sense of unity or support, and restores a healthy perspective on a given situation. Everyone wants to work in an environment that is as tension free as possible, where they feel accepted, supported, and able to develop a healthy perspective on the difficulties they inevitably face as working people. It is quite common for leaders and people who write about leadership to say that leaders must have a sense of humor. But exactly what does this mean? Although humor can make a positive contribution to the work environment, some types of humor are inappropriate.

Clearly, humor should never be used in a way that causes anyone discomfort. It is commonly understood that jokes about sex, religion, or politics are not appropriate. Many people are very uncomfortable with sexual innuendo in the workplace. In addition, such comments could be construed as sexual harassment. Obviously, jokes about a person's appearance or "bathroom" humor are also inappropriate on the job. So, if a leader is supposed to use humor, what can he or she joke about? The safest and most effective humor to use in the work setting is humor that pokes fun at one's own flaws, neuroses, and inadequacies. When a leader makes these jokes, people are brought closer together because they can relate to what the leader is talking about. Humor works when it is clever, creative, and considerate.

Humor also has to do with self-acceptance—the wry, knowing smile that recognizes "I am only human." Writer Steven Covey (1989) lists a sense of humor as one of his characteristics of principle-centered leaders by stating that strong leaders "have a healthy sense of humor, particularly laughing at themselves and not at others' expense" (p. 232). The more important the person, the more meaningful the self-deprecating humor. Poking fun at oneself and generally not taking oneself too seriously is a leadership trait that helps create a climate where people feel relaxed and creative.

Humor can facilitate communication, build relationships, reduce stress, provide perspective, and energize a group. Humor offers a nonthreatening way for employees to communicate with others and avoid strong emotions. In addition, humor can develop staff cohesion and a team effort. Humor is a great stress reliever because it makes people feel good—and it is difficult to feel good and feel stress at the same time (Sultanoff, 1993).

SUMMARY

Leaders-in-training must have opportunities to learn about multiple leadership theories, to reflect on them, and to explore the benefits of using these theories as a framework for solving real problems in the school setting. As prospective leaders develop proficiency in leadership standards, neither universities nor school districts alone can provide both exposure to the content knowledge and supervised guided practice over time. Clearly, it is not a matter of theory or practice—a marriage of both is needed. As our four critical players work on the concerns before them, it is likely each will have cause to reflect on leadership theory and practices that could influence their decisions regarding which actions will bring the most positive resolution for all stakeholders.

4

Collaborative Partnerships for Preparing Leaders

Perhaps what university programs need to have is more field people who will work with us.

—G. Ivory & M. Acker-Hocevar (2005)

The only thing constant is change itself, and the rate at which change occurs is increasing rapidly—most of us have said those or similar words more than once. We accept that the world we prepare students to live in will be very different from the one we know, but sometimes those closest to an issue are the last to see it clearly. Perhaps that explains the

---

Material from Ivory, G., & Acker-Hocevar, M. (2005). *Voices from the Field: Phase 3.* Superintendent focus group interview transcripts. Texas: University Council for Educational Administration. Used with permission.

Material from Gustafson, D. M. (2005). *A Case Study of a Professional Administrative Leadership Academy*. Unpublished doctoral dissertation, Kansas State University, Manhattan. Used with permission.

defensive uproar in response to recent voices critical of training programs for school administrators.

The changes in expectations of leaders produce a new definition of leadership. Why, then, would it surprise anyone that the traditional preparation program for school leaders can no longer adequately prepare educators for leadership roles? We expect preparation programs to produce effective leaders. In a domino-like effect, when expectations of leadership change, a redesigning of preparation programs is inevitable. Otherwise, we continue doing what we have always done, getting the kind of leaders we have always gotten, leaders whose training no longer matches the leadership challenges ahead. If we are not "re-visioning" leadership and appropriate preparation now, we are way behind.

In a recent national study of 28 schools and departments of education, researchers found "the overall quality of educational administration programs in the United States to be poor," the typical curriculum to be "a nearly random collection of courses," and the programs to "lack rigor and fail to focus on the core business of the schools—learning and teaching" (Levine, 2005, pp. 23–30). In the midst of the defensive responses to critics, we acknowledge the need to redesign programs that prepare school leaders. School leaders themselves have told us, "My preparation program didn't prepare me for this!" And even if past preparation programs had been perfect and had successfully prepared leaders for today, we should be looking at changes in order to prepare school leaders for tomorrow. The good news is that we can prepare leaders for this new vision of leadership—but not without substantial changes to the preparation programs on which we have relied in the past. The essential characteristics of such a partnership were described by Gunn (2000, as cited in Funk, 2005): (1) teachers with knowledge of leading and ability to instruct others in the art, (2) students who want to learn about leadership and believe that instruction in leadership can help them be more effective, and (3) a curriculum developed and transmitted through a variety of instructional strategies.

We suggest that the teachers we need in the leadership preparation program for school leaders include both those with knowledge of theory and those now performing as successful leaders in our schools. We believe that leaders-in-training are looking for a blend of theory and skills that will enable them to meet today's educational challenges. And we are convinced by our own positive experiences that by working together, university and school district leaders can design a curriculum that includes an expanded knowledge base and meaningful instructional strategies for applying that knowledge. This chapter describes the process for merging theory and practice, what partnerships look like, and why the model works.

THE CASE FOR MERGING THEORY/PRACTICE

Strong educational leaders can be developed by a three-stage process of knowledge and theory acquisition, guided practice, and individual and group reflection. Such concurrent activities do not fit in the structure of leadership preparation programs typically in place today. Knowledge and theory acquisition is the forte of the university. To accomplish the remaining two stages, guided practice and individual and group reflection on the leadership process, an additional dimension is required. The university needs a partner in order for participants to learn from each other in a series of interchanging teaching and learning roles and to give all participants a stronger understanding of leadership itself. If all participants are to have a range of meaningful experiences to draw from as they grow professionally, leaders operating successfully in the schools today must be part of the preparation program. Partnerships between universities and school districts make it possible to merge theory and practices. However, putting this in place will require both the university and the school district to make significant changes.

The University's Perspective

First, those of us at the university must accept the fact that the traditional administrator preparation training models are no longer effective in preparing leaders to succeed in the high-stakes-accountability world that currently exists. The traditional modes of leadership preparation will not work in this time of multiple groups of vocal, articulate, empowered constituents: staff, parents, students, communities, and state and federal legislators. Leaders today need to know how to ask the right questions, to take a systems-thinking approach, to determine the correct responses from a plethora of options, and to develop and engage all stakeholders in dynamic and continuous professional learning communities. Leaders today need to be quiet and humble, yet also strong, uninterested in gaining power for themselves, willing to be led as well as to lead, and willing to visibly work as hard as those who work with them. These are the "Level 5 leaders" Collins described in *Good to Great* (2001), a book based on leadership models of successful corporations.

What we need is a new philosophy for grounding the new preparation programs—one focused on creating (1) collaborative systems that link all stakeholders both vertically and horizontally and (2) leaders who can build the leadership capacity of the organization and its members. The previous chapters of this book delineate new expectations for leadership that bring people together, rather than isolate or exclude. This new model of leadership must be nonhierarchical and based on growth at all levels of the organization. It must be characterized by leaders sharing power, rather than holding on to it.

Current structures and practices must be understood in order to make significant changes. Many university and public school staff members are trapped within traditional systems that make it very difficult to create new forms of leadership preparation. University leadership preparation programs have long been strong in theories about learning and change but are often less connected to the real-world settings of schools. Initiating reform requires suspending traditional practices in order to allow a new format to emerge—one that has rigor and is customized to fit university, district, and student needs and prepares exemplary leaders in both organizations. University staff will need to develop rapport and trust with their public school partners; likewise, public school partners will need to develop rapport and trust with their university partners.

The advent of the No Child Left Behind Act of 2001 (NCLB) legislation has radically changed the world for public schools, but the accountability movement is just beginning to move upward into higher education, through the efforts of accrediting systems such as the National Commission for Accrediting Teacher Education (NCATE) and the North Central Association (NCA). Thus university instructors without recent experience in schools or with high-stakes accountability are even further removed from school issues. Traditional course requirements and degree programs have changed very little in the past 20 years, despite their existence within a rapidly changing world, especially demographically and technologically. Instead of moving closer to the heart of the school system as they train school leaders, most university preparation programs appear to have moved away from those settings. The Levine (2005) researchers found that much of the curriculum of education programs was "outdated and based on school experiences from the distant past" (p. 31).

In response to the indictment of traditional preparation programs, Jerome Murphy (2006) offered three challenges for those who would work to resolve the problems of administrative preparation programs:

1. A balanced, dual teaching mission of preparing researchers and practitioners
2. A research agenda designed to inform and improve practice
3. Open lines of communication between discipline-oriented and profession-oriented faculty. (pp. 530–531)

We propose a model for university and school partnerships that provides the structure for addressing these challenges.

The View From the School District

School personnel are struggling with the issues of the times and with new pressures of avoiding sanctions related to meeting the NCLB requirements. As they face multiple challenges each day, many school leaders are in a survival mode, struggling just to keep up. They have little time to reflect or to think about which theories are behind their practices—or which theories might improve practice. When teachers begin taking graduate courses in leadership to increase their knowledge base, salaries, and/or ability to succeed with their students, they often find that coursework has little connection to their real world of school. Being a leader in their world means guiding, instructing, supporting, and nurturing the individual members of an entire school community through a maelstrom of change in their lives, while preparing each of them for the future.

Schools are being held accountable for the success of all students and for raising student performance to the highest level ever. Leaders today need to be well trained in strategies to make such student performance possible; they need ways to build leadership capacity in the organization and in all the stakeholders, because it is no longer possible to be the lone leader and succeed. Many preparation programs are missing the mark.

TIME FOR A NEW MODEL

The factory system design of today's schools was created to produce students who could follow rules, ask few questions, and know that there was always one right answer. The world of the twenty-first century is much different, and that factory model is ill-suited for preparing students for a successful future. However, there is hope. The situation existing in education today, as demands are made for changes and the demographic shift looms, with fewer and fewer teacher or administrator candidates on the horizon, provides a unique opportunity and need for schools and universities to work together. It is time for a new collaborative model that blends the talents of both organizations. Murphy (2006) affirmed the importance of current timing:

> Now is the time for Ed [*sic*] Schools to experiment with bold new approaches . . . to challenge the stifling insularity that marks this field and to think in novel new ways about leadership education . . . time for Ed Schools to capitalize on this moment of discontent. (p. 536)

A new model for preparing school leaders must bring theory and practice together in new, more viable ways. It must combine teaching and learning at all levels, and it must produce simultaneous, ongoing professional growth for both universities and public schools. School and university partnerships, a unique blending of the strengths of both, are emerging as the structure that offers the greatest potential for preparing strong leaders for the future. These collaborative partnerships present an opportunity for the two organizations to reconnect and revitalize leadership preparation and school leadership itself. In essence, it is time for a renaissance—a radical change in substance and style of administrator preparation programs. Exemplary university-school partnerships for training a new breed of leaders merge theory with practice by collaboratively developing a long-term, individualized, integrated, and spiraling curriculum;

fostering habits of reflective practice; incorporating authentic assessment of performance; and including supervised internship experiences that allow the roles of teacher and learner to be interchangeable among students, trainers, planners, and mentors.

Becoming leaders suited to the educational environment today requires knowledge of theory—and a vision of what that theory looks like when put into use in a real school. Meaningful experiences must allow leaders-in-training to practice, reflect, refine, and revise, until finally given full responsibility for leadership. Neither the university setting nor the schools alone can bring all of those components together. What better solution than partnerships between the two for merging theory and practice! We offer a model we call *partnership academies for leaders.*

PARTNERSHIP ACADEMIES FOR LEADERS

The partnership academy for leaders model of leadership preparation is based upon a close connection between theory and practice. Practice must be theory driven. However, theory must be continually tested in the real world of schools. The partnership academy model allows professors, administrators, and leaders-in-training to learn from one another. It is based upon the assumption that leaders are needed at all levels of the organization. Some partnership academy programs focus on preparing new school administrators; others focus on enhancing the leadership abilities of current administrators; and still others focus on the leadership structure of classroom teachers.

In designing partnership academies for leaders, we look to the medical, law, and teacher preparation models. Just as teacher education has changed, so must leader training change to more closely reflect the realities of real administration. Historically, prospective teachers entered classrooms for the first time toward the end of the third year of college, when they spent a few weeks observing and assisting with routine tasks. In the final year of a four-year program, they "student taught" half days for one semester in a classroom with a master teacher. The teachers-in-training were seldom left alone in the classroom, and teaching responsibilities were generally limited to discrete lessons, with considerable direction from the supervising teacher. Students in the classes knew who the "real" teacher in the room was and reacted accordingly within the already-established classroom management system put in place earlier by the supervising teacher. The contrast between this setting and that first day on the job in the real world was substantial!

Good teacher-training programs today look very different. Many now use the *professional development school* (PDS) model, which is a partnership between university programs that prepare teachers and school districts that open their classrooms for meaningful, real-world experiences for these teachers-in-training. PDS programs typically place students in classrooms as observers early on in the student's training and continue direct involvement with increasing levels of responsibility throughout the four-year program. Teachers-in-training observe, assist, and reflect on what they see successful teachers do. This culminates in an experience that places the student as an *intern* (notice the shift from the label *student teacher*) with major teaching responsibilities in the final year. Partnership academies for leaders build on the strengths of the PDS models (NCATE, 2006).

Regardless of the individual focus, partnership academies for leaders share these characteristics:

1. Collaborative planning
2. An integrated, spiraling curriculum
3. Field experiences
4. A mentoring component

Collaborative Planning

A partnership academy for leaders is based on active participation of the partners in an ongoing collaborative planning process. The collaboration begins with the determination of the purpose for the partnership—something that is important to the partners, such as preparing new administrators, enhancing skills of present administrators, or building teacher leadership. The partners collaboratively design a format compatible with their respective calendars and reasonably workable for prospective participants, whom they recognize will have full-time classroom teaching assignments or support roles in the district at the same time they are participating in the academy. This opportunity to design a program format that best meets the needs of partners and participants is a great advantage of the partnership approach. The partners continue to collaborate on decisions about curriculum, assessment, activities, and rewards for participants throughout the extent of the academy.

District leaders today are hungry for resources, research-based practices, and professional growth opportunities for staff at all levels. Universities are under attack for their lack of connectivity to public schools and need avenues for staff to maintain deeper understanding of how real schools function. The collaborative partnership is a model whereby mutual needs can be resolved and the two organizations strengthened.

Integrated, Spiraling Curriculum

Instead of a sequence of discrete courses that constitute the curriculum in the traditional leadership preparation program, the course of study for the partnership academies for leaders integrates the content and regularly reintroduces it in ever-increasing levels of understanding and application, known as a *spiraling curriculum.* In effect, all of the courses are being taught all the time, all the way through the program. Students are introduced to leadership knowledge, experience introductory field experiences, and, when ready, are expected to demonstrate competency with increasingly greater degrees of responsibility.

Based on the collaborative planning of the partners, the integrated, spiraling curriculum is delivered in a mixture of face-to-face group interaction, online asynchronous communication that brings people together at the same time across distances, online communication that allows participants to work at their own time and pace, and frequent field experiences that allow participants to apply new knowledge in the context of real practice, under the guidance of trained mentors who are successful leaders. An important feature of this model is that both the university and school planners are constantly collaborating to monitor, revise, customize, and connect concepts as the program progresses.

The length of the partnership academy program depends on the requirements for which the partners agree to be responsible. A degree may be awarded for successful program completion; eligibility for state licensure may be the targeted outcome; or some combination of degree and licensure may be achieved. Such programs are generally about two years long, including summer work. Partnerships that target teacher leadership recognize that more and more teachers are interested in leading in meaningful and important ways, while staying in classroom positions. Table 4.1, "Examples of Partnership Models," describes possible partnership academy formats. Whatever the form or label, partners for preparing leaders must be true to basic concepts similar to those in the PDS model. The integrated, spiraling curriculum is described in more detail in Chapter 5.

The Mentoring Component

Leaders-in-training benefit most when they are assigned to a mentor, a successful leader who is practicing good leadership. In the partnership academies for leaders model, this is more than a buddy system or an invitation to "call when you have a question." The most effective academies give a structure to the mentor-mentee relationship. There are clear expectations for periodic connections between the mentor and the leader-in-training (see Resource J). The mentor accepts responsibility for guiding the trainee through appropriate field experiences. The district takes the lead in assigning mentors, matching academy students with practitioners who have the skills and professional expertise desired of district administrators. A series of mentors can be assigned to oversee specific field-based projects determined collaboratively by the student, immediate supervisor, and mentor, or one mentor can be assigned to work with one student throughout the entire academy.

The selection and matching of strong, growth-oriented mentors is important. Mentors need to understand and support the development of

Table 4.1 Examples of Partnership Models

Each partnership has unique groupings, purposes, length, and outcomes. These descriptions are examples from actual academy experiences. Students in these academies attend part time, with full-time teaching responsibilities within their districts.

Partners	*Purposes*	*Length*	*Outcomes*
One District, One University	Professional growth for practicing administrators	Varied	College and/or local inservice credit
Three Districts, One University	Address administrative shortages; change current training model	2 years	College credit, MS degree, and building-level licensure
Two Districts, One University	Train a group of teacher and/or administrative leaders, with a focus on high-performance teaming	2.5 years	College credit, MS degree, and/or building licensure
One District, One University	Develop teacher leaders for a variety of district and building positions	2 years	College credit, MS degree, additional hours required for building-leader licensure
Two Districts, One University, Distance Learning Model	Develop teacher and/or administrative leaders to address shortages, with a focus on technology and diversity	2 years	College credit, MS degree, additional hours required for building-leader licensure
One District, One University	Develop educational leaders for building and district levels, with a focus on closing the achievement gap	2 years	College credit, MS degree, additional hours required for building-leader licensure
One District, One University, Distance Learning Model	Develop educational leaders for building and district levels	2 years	College credit, MS degree, additional hours required for building-leader licensure
Several Districts, One University, Distance Learning Model	Develop educational leaders for building and district levels	2 years	College credit, MS degree, additional hours required for building-leader licensure

leaders-in-training and believe in and be skilled at collaboration. Past documented leadership should be a component of each mentor's background. Mentors can be drawn from within the district or from the university and perhaps from leadership within the community. It is helpful to have one of the mentors serve as "lead mentor," to coordinate the work of all the mentors throughout the academy, keep them apprised of the entire project and internship activities, and assist them in becoming a supportive network resource for each other.

FIELD EXPERIENCES

Partnership academies give leaders-in-training immediate opportunities to apply theory and knowledge in authentic settings under the guidance of qualified mentors. Traditional preparation programs include blocks of internship experiences, usually toward the end of the two-year leadership preparation program. As a result, connections between the theory encountered in the classroom and the experience in the field are less than clear, or even absent. At best, the internship is a narrow slice, not representative of the overall scope of successful performance of the school leader. Researchers reported field experiences to be the weakest element in preparation programs they reviewed (Bottoms, O'Neill, Fry, & Hill, 2003). Too often, standards for content and rigor of these experiences do not exist, and there is no system of accountability for ensuring that standards are followed. The rigor of internships varies with the instructor and the district liaison. While concern over the quality of internship experiences is not new, agreement on the importance of application experiences in training programs is stronger than ever.

When practice is merged with theory in a partnership academy program, the leader-in-training can apply new knowledge in authentic settings from the onset and continually throughout the length of the program. As leadership theory is encountered and strategies for being a good leader are studied, the leader-in-training begins working with the support of a master practitioner to connect related performance skills and strategies for leading in an authentic setting. This spiraling blend of learning and application with increasing degrees of leadership responsibility results in a direct and immediate connection of theory to real practice.

Applying theory to practice in this fashion creates the potential for giving attention to particular skill levels attained and the developmental progress of the learner. Just as we differentiate instruction to accommodate learners in our classrooms, field experiences and the preparation program itself can be adjusted as the program proceeds, depending on the needs of the learners and the changing conditions of the situation in the partnering school district. Skills that are well established become the foundation for stretching learners to the next level of proficiency. As experiences in the real world of schools change, so can the context of field applications for the leaders-in-training. Imagine the changes that would have been made if a partnership preparation program like this had been in place as NCLB requirements arrived in the real world of school leadership.

WHY THE NEW MODEL WORKS

Professional academies for leaders are effective for a number of reasons. By watching practitioners focus on learning and observing how they make positive differences on student achievement, leaders-in-training form a clear picture of successful practices for leading school improvement. They observe these efforts over time, participate in various stages of the process, and benefit from individual and collective reflections on what they have observed. Leaders-in-training learn from their own failures and successes, as well as from those of mentors and other practitioners. They have time to learn about and identify actual performance of simple, basic practices that research tells us are essential to success as a leader. Then, they have an opportunity to practice building their own skills under the guidance of a successful leader. As skills are developed, the academy program can be adapted to accommodate individual professional growth and district needs for leadership. Reading about how to lead professional learning communities is helpful to the leader-in-training. Practicing the skill is powerful. When knowledge and content development are followed by observation, participation, responsibility, and reflection, professional growth is most likely to occur.

At the same time, partnership academies give the district direct access to the latest research on best practice. University partners are introducing leaders-in-training to theory and the latest research on best practice. The leaders-in-training are talking with mentors about the research and theory most closely related to what is happening in the schools where they work. In assisting mentees with field experiences to apply this information, mentors themselves reflect on current practice, expand their own professional expertise, and make even greater positive differences in their own areas of responsibility. As practitioners combine their skills in practice with the knowledge from research on best practice, they initiate conversations with district colleagues and university members of the partnership team. Imagine the contribution this makes to the culture of the school district and to the understanding university staff have of what practice really looks like in schools. The designs of other university programs are altered, and that gap between preparation and the real world narrows.

Watching leaders create an environment that builds relationships and encourages leadership throughout the system gives leaders-in-training an invaluable learning experience. Principals should be judged as successful not on the basis of programs put in place, but on the basis of how many new leaders are emerging. Little chance for large-scale reform exists unless capacity building is occurring throughout the system at all levels (Fullan, 2005). The importance of leadership at all levels, distributive leadership, and capacity building has been addressed by many educational researchers (Elmore, 2000; Lambert, 2003; Spillane, 2006). Designers of preparation programs for school and district leaders must attend to these messages, especially if we are also to support the professional growth of practicing leaders in positions now. Lessons about the research on leader behaviors that encourage leadership in others (at all levels) as well as guiding future leaders in removing barriers to building leadership capacity are included in the scope of all academy preparation programs. Experiences with mentors and frequent opportunities to practice skills related to building leadership capacity in others help new leaders and current practitioners recognize the importance of this concept and plan their own efforts to accomplish the necessary reform.

Partnership academies are formed for the purpose of designing and delivering preparation programs that give prospective leaders knowledge of important theory and best practice, putting them in place in real school settings. When theory and practice merge, the leaders-in-training work directly with practicing administrators who act as formal mentors, often for an extended period of time. To prepare leaders for their future roles, experiences of increasing levels of responsibility over the two-year program enable them to learn, practice, reflect, refine, and grow professionally. It is important to note that instilling this *learn-practice-reflect-refine-grow* process is as important an objective in preparing leaders as the content and skills gained from the activity itself.

BENEFITS TO THE PARTNERS

We have already mentioned some of the benefits that accrue to both partners when universities and school districts collaborate to bring theory and practice closer together. Other direct benefits to the partners are shown below. The lists look different, but the benefits are mutual and overlapping in many respects.

Districts benefit in at least these important ways:

1. Selection of participants in the program
2. Influencing the curriculum content and participating in its delivery
3. Increasing the number of qualified applicants for leader positions
4. Professional growth of participants and district staff

Universities benefit directly in at least these ways:

1. Increased enrollment of prospective leaders with high potential
2. Visibility as an effective resource in the educational community
3. Opportunities to build other partnerships
4. Networking with school leader practitioners

District leaders typically do not even know when staff members first enroll in traditional preparation programs, as in most cases no recommendation from an employer is necessary or invited. In contrast, districts approve which staff members will participate in partnership academies for leaders. District leaders also have the opportunity to encourage emerging leaders to pursue a preparation program. The influence of supervisors has been identified as a major factor in the decision teachers make to pursue a career in administration (Zacharakis, Devin, & Miller, 2006). The quotes below are from teachers describing why they decided to apply for admission to a partnership preparation program:

> If the academy brochure had just been put in my box at school, I would have never done anything with it. However, my former principal came and talked to me personally and said, "This is for you; you need to do this." She knew I wanted to start on a masters but she also knew I just wasn't doing it. So she saw this as an opportunity for me to get started. I really didn't even hesitate; I just did it. (Gustafson, 2005, p. 96)

> My principal told everyone in the building about the academy opportunity, and then she came around personally to those she thought were ready for such an experience. As we talked about it, I liked the idea of a hands-on learning opportunity more than sitting in class all the time. I already have a graduate degree but I had thought about getting building certification. (Gustafson, 2005, p. 104)

In partnership academies, the partners collaboratively design the application and screening process to best meet needs expressed by both partners. The district determines how the academy can best support its priorities and designs a selection process that identifies those most likely to become leaders of those efforts. While an increase in student enrollment numbers may be the most visible result, university partners also benefit when all students are selected on the basis of agreed-upon measures of potential for success.

District partners enjoy considerable influence over the content of the curriculum and its delivery. In this manner, planners make sure the skills the district values most will be emphasized in the preparation of future leaders. The university benefits by clarifying its vision of what schools need from preparation programs. Both partners see the program as a way to make sure there are a greater number of qualified applicants for future positions as they occur. District leaders recognize the benefit from the opportunity to see the leader-in-training grow during the extent of the preparation program—much like an extensive interview! When graduates of the academy programs apply for positions, they have documented evidence of their proficiency in a leadership role, which gives district leaders more information to bring to decisions about selection and assignment of new personnel.

District partners discover that interaction between leaders-in-training and practicing mentors proves to be a strong professional growth activity for leaders already in the field. The line separating teaching and learning becomes intentionally blurred. The mentor has dual responsibilities of being a teacher and a learner. As mentors guide and support leaders-in-training, they become more aware of their own skills and the professional growth they need to carry out their respective assignments. They learn mentoring skills that are important for supporting teachers and employees in other parts of the school operation. Finally, they are presented with the effectiveness of the learn-practice-reflect-refine-grow cycle themselves, and their own performance is enhanced. University staff partners report similar benefits from their involvement in partnership activities. As professional growth occurs across the district and with university staff, new ideas form for new collaborative projects.

Partners join forces because they believe they can gain greater benefit from working together than working separately. It is past time for those of us who work in educational leadership preparation programs to join forces with practitioners for the greater benefit of all. Certainly, there has always been a connection of some sort between us. After all, practitioners are the products of our programs: We know them, and they know us. However, we really haven't paid enough attention to whether our products—present leaders—felt our programs prepared them for the challenges they face as practitioners. The discussions have too often been limited to choosing a side in a debate supporting theory or supporting practice. In partnership academies for leaders, both theory and practice are integral parts of the preparation program.

THE IMPACT OF POLITICS ON LEADERSHIP

Politics does not have to be a negative term. If we use this term to describe the "hidden rules" (Payne, 1996) of success, few would disagree that there is an art of politics involved in successful leadership. Most school and district leaders can share stories about times they used political skills and experienced positive outcomes—and they can likely recount other examples of political influences contributing to negative outcomes. The best place to learn the politics of the education business is in the field. In partnership academies, authentic and frequent applications of leadership skills provide the opportunity for leaders-in-training to have such experiences, reflect on them in a nonthreatening environment, and build skills for future field interactions.

ENDURING QUALITIES OF COLLABORATIVE PARTNERSHIPS

The challenge of finding a way to bring theory and practice together is reason enough to support a renaissance of preparation programs, which have long been perceived as lacking connectedness to the realities of leading in public schools. A greater challenge, however, is doing that in a manner that addresses the gap of reality now and prevents its recurrence in the future. We can be assured that the process of change will not stop. New research will provide more information that will be helpful to practitioners, and changing conditions around us will create new expectations for school leaders. It is not enough to address the gap we see between preparation programs and successful practice now. We need a model that can change with the times and will not produce the same problem in the future.

To find out how to improve productivity, quality, and performance, we should involve the people who do the work (Drucker, 1991). One of the greatest benefits of the collaborative partnership model is the partnership itself. By partnering with those closest to the work, both universities and public schools can be confident that the preparation program in place will be as dynamic and fluid as the real world around it. Working together, we access research and best practices; apply, analyze, synthesize, and evaluate new solutions in authentic settings; and collaborate in dynamic, continuous professional growth experiences that revitalize both the educational systems and those who work in them. As change occurs in school leadership practices in the real world, the partners adjust the preparation content and context. Rigorous standards can continue even though the people, resources, and situations change over time. Partnership academies for leaders sustain a tight connection between universities and schools. We find the collaborative partnership model to be the surest approach to minimizing the gap between theory and practice.

Theory is important. It adds meaning to what happens in real schools on an everyday basis. It helps us understand why something worked—or didn't work. Used correctly, theory *informs* practice. However, in the midst of daily, often unscheduled events in real schools, leaders must call on more than theory to survive. Knowing *how to apply* what we learn from theory and having the *performance skills* to do that can be practiced and tested only in authentic settings in the real world. Partnerships are the perfect blend of opportunities for leaders-in-training to apply theory in the setting of the new vision for leadership described earlier.

Knowing that leadership makes a difference is not enough information for leaders-in-training. They must be prepared to do what works in the field. The following questions need to be answered:

- What do principals do that makes the positive difference in student performance?
- How do they carry out basic practices of leadership?
- What does it look like to lead professional learning communities?
- How do they build leadership throughout the system?

SUMMARY

Preparation must include knowing how to put into practice the theories and knowledge emerging from research. The partnership academies for leaders model can drive the redesigning of preparation programs for leaders—bringing together the knowledge and theory of the traditional preparation program and the reality of what leaders do each day as they successfully practice in the real world. In partnership academies, universities and schools work together, sharing their respective expertise and experiences to answer critical questions for leaders-in-training.

All players in our four scenarios benefit from the marriage of theory and practice in preparation programs. The superintendent in the district leadership role receives support for guiding the professional growth and building the leadership capacity at the district level; the principal grows as a mentor and as a practitioner and builds the leadership capacity at the building level. The district functions better at all levels as it has improved access to pertinent research and as the university partner shares that information. The professor receives the benefit from a closer connection to the world as it actually looks in schools today and a recognition that students are prepared for the real world. The leader-in-training benefits from having a collaborative program that uses practice to inform theory and theory to inform practice. The mutual benefit of this collaboration is a priceless return from merging theory and practice.

5

Redesigning the Curriculum to Match the New Realities

Real life is the best curriculum. . . . The curriculum for the 21st century must be based on reality, not on "disciplines" and textbooks.

—B. Kovalik (1994)

When school districts and administrator preparation programs form partnerships, an opportunity is created to reshape the most influential part of the preparation program—the curriculum itself. Just as students do not meet life in discrete units by subject area or by course title in their first years on the job, novice administrators face dilemmas that are rarely simple or one-dimensional. The ability to blend all they have learned from many sources guides leaders in working through real-life problems. Unfortunately, the most recent research describing the curriculum used for preparing our nation's educational leaders reports it as more like a random group of courses related to a past that no longer exists (Levine, 2005).

Quality preparation programs must match new realities of schooling, which require an integration of theory and practice. An integrated, spiraling curriculum allows university and school district leaders to collaboratively customize the curriculum to include essential student learning for both types of organizations, allows students multiple opportunities to apply their learning to actual practice, and provides multiple opportunities for students to reflect regularly on research-based best practices. In this chapter, we briefly describe the traditional curriculum design, followed by an alternate curriculum design used in partnership academies for leaders. Critical skills for today's educational leaders are defined and described: problem-solving frameworks, conflict resolution skills, situational awareness, and resiliency skills. We have also included sections on reflective practice; individualized, supervised field experiences; and performance assessment—additional elements that are embedded in the integrated, spiraling curriculum for partnership academies for leaders.

TRADITIONAL CURRICULUM DESIGN

In the past, preparation program curricula consisted of discrete courses, delivered in a recommended sequence by university professors in specified content areas that have changed little over the past 20 years. There was little, if any, coordination between courses and little or no coordination between the content in these courses. Any field experiences included in the preparation program were often a result of students thinking of something on their own and providing bits of documentation, such as attendance logs or supervisor approval forms. In this fragmented presentation of traditional preparation programs, students with high ability may have been able to see connections and develop quality field experiences on their own. However, such connections were unlikely and rarely included supervisors or mentors with enough knowledge of the students or the course content to provide true guidance. Any mentors involved were rarely connected to the university program and were most likely the product of traditional preparation programs, with no training for mentoring. The chance of a leader-in-training receiving a coordinated, seamless preparation for the future has been quite small.

CURRICULUM DESIGN IN PARTNERSHIPS

A suggested criteria for excellence in curriculum for preparing educational leaders resulted from the Levine (2005) research: "rigorous, coherent, and organized to teach the skills and knowledge needed by leaders at specific types of schools, and at the various stages of their careers; integrates the theory and practice of administrations" (p. 58). Leaders-in-training need a framework for leadership and then ongoing, long-term opportunities to practice applying that framework to authentic settings and situations—an integrated, spiraling curriculum. This type of training continues throughout the partnership preparation programs, in increasingly more rigorous tests of leadership proficiency.

In partnership academies for leaders, staff in both universities and schools (or all, if a consortium is involved) (1) influence the content and the delivery of the experiences to meet higher standards for preparation programs and (2) provide a blend of theory, research, and best practices in a rigorous, engaging, performance-based fashion. These programs include the ability to organize learning and field experiences in a more integrated fashion that provides real-world experiences for the application and evaluation of theories and best practices. Coursework is supported by appropriate and individualized field-based experiences to develop increasing proficiency over time in all of the collaboratively developed standards.

In an integrated, spiraling curriculum, aspiring educational leaders are engaged in blending their learning about administrative leadership as new ideas are encountered. Concepts are introduced by university and district planners and then become the foundation for the application of administrative leadership skills in real settings, with time allotted for analysis and reflection. This spiraling-curriculum approach allows instructors to continue to reinforce the concepts, moving gradually to higher levels of understanding and mastery, revealing new aspects and increasingly rigorous levels of theory and application. Students then process the material at higher levels of awareness, application, and expertise.

Students in administrator preparation programs must prepare for the real problems they will encounter in schools, in the way they will face them in real life. Today's educational leaders are inundated with several issues at one time on a daily basis. They do not have discrete, isolated, artificial problems, as often presented in traditional preparation programs. Therefore, the preparation curriculum should not be taught in discrete units, but in an integrated and applied fashion. In partnership academies, each time a concept is presented, students and planners share their prior experience in similar settings and improve upon previous reactions and recommendations. Students bring with them a rich experience base, as do the planners. A real-world, integrated, spiraling curriculum allows each participant to share and explore those experiences, to both teach and learn throughout the length of the program.

This type of brain-compatible learning consists mostly of "concepts, skills, and attitudes/values that students can experience through *being there*" (Kovalik, 1994, p. xvi). This curriculum is student centered and can be customized for each learner (differentiated instruction), because the learning is designed around actual school settings and individual assignments. Students process curriculum concepts and apply them to their own settings, followed by evaluation and reflection. This process reduces "telling" and increases exploration, discovery, and application of concepts to the real world (Kovalik, 1994). Kovalik's theories on integrated curricula have been strongly reinforced by newer studies related to brain research and the learning brain that define intelligence as "an integrated process . . . the various dimensions of intelligence have evolved together, are dependent on one another, and are designed to work in concert" (Dickmann, Stanford-Blair,

& Rosati-Bojar, 2004, pp. 12–13). Leaders-in-training also need individual experiences that allow them to create, or construct, their own learning and leadership structures, experiences that are ongoing and continuous and allow ample time for reflection and adjustments. The immediate application of theory in partnership academies allows students the time and information for processing, each in their own fashion.

Clearly, an ability to customize the training program is a definite advantage provided by the integrated, spiraling curriculum that addresses the growing demands for differentiated instruction. A long-term (two or more years with frequent, regular meetings) degree or licensure partnership program meets several recommendations from the Levine (2005) research, calling for the redesigning of educational leadership programs, similar to the two-year master's degree in business administration. An extended term allows adequate time for individual reflection on and processing of the integrated, spiraling curriculum by both teachers and students.

There are other important elements of this spiraling curriculum, often overlooked as priorities. "The measure of an effective principal has changed and a new set of skills is required to create an environment where every child is successful" (Devin, 2004, p. 74). Today's leaders must be prepared to create that environment for success wherever they serve. Examples of new skills that should be a continuous part of the spiraling curriculum, and are necessary for today's leaders, are described below. Ideally, readers can appreciate the advantages an integrated, spiraling curriculum provides over a more traditional program in satisfying concerns for current leadership preparation programs.

Practicing leaders and leaders-in-training need to be acquainted with current findings of leadership studies, both from the educational field and outside of education. Many businesses today are also dealing with a high degree of change and increased accountability and can provide parallel research and strategies for working with and leading stakeholders in such times. The university brings to a partnership academy the capacity for meeting this expectation for current research, leadership frameworks, and best practices. Obviously, the breadth of leadership research is expanding daily, and planners need to constantly read and update resources and references to remain current. Familiarity with educational labs and educational research Web sites is a must for both university and school practitioners. School partners also have access to many state and district resources as well as networking possibilities for reviewing and revising educational leadership theories.

Leaders-in-training also need to develop practical skills that will enhance their performance as they blend theory and practice. Problems and conflicts appear daily; thus a problem-solving framework and conflict resolution skills are embedded in the partnership academy curriculum from the beginning of the program. Situational awareness and resiliency skills are included so students will have the skills needed to lead their stakeholders with courage and develop the stamina required to support and sustain organizations through rapid change.

PROBLEM-SOLVING FRAMEWORK

New principals are often amazed by the amount of time spent on helping others get along, on resolving minor issues when so many major issues are also on their plates. A method of assigning priority levels is needed to guide novice administrators in learning to walk into crisis situations, assess the problems and needs, consider ramifications of possible solutions, and then take action to gain the best possible results for students, with minimal political damage. The spiraling curriculum in partnership academies includes a basic problem-solving framework that can be used by new administrators to confront the often life-altering situations they may face on a regular basis. These frameworks can be pulled from other careers, such as the medical triage model used in most emergency rooms; creative problem-solving models that exist in business and industry can also be used. Many districts have put in place building extensive problem-solving frameworks as part of their work to improve student performance in math. An example of a basic framework that could be applied in several settings is included here:

1. Determine the essential problem.
2. Gather information and generate alternative solutions.
3. Develop the criteria for selection.
4. Evaluate and rate the alternatives, based on the criteria.
5. Develop an action plan using the selected solution.
6. Repeat the process (since inevitably, new problems will arise).

This framework is loosely based upon the work of Treffinger and Isaksen (1992, as cited in Adams & Pierce, 2006, p. 352) on creative problem solving, a process used for over 20 years as a process to develop solutions for tough problems.

The curricula in partnership academies allow university and district practitioners to work together to structure opportunities for leaders-in-training to practice developing workable solutions to real-world problems, by using a standard framework throughout the length of their preparation programs and in their own settings. As the students become more proficient in solving problems, they are able to handle increasing levels of difficulty. Engagement increases because they are resolving real problems (with supervision).

CONFLICT RESOLUTION SKILLS

Conflict resolution skills are also a part of the academy curriculum, needed as new leaders find themselves mediating a variety of daily conflicts with parents, students, staff, and community members. Many conflict resolution training programs in business and education exist today in response to the tumultuous times we live in. Most school districts offer conflict mediation training, negotiations, and bargaining workshops. In partnership academies, there are available curriculum resources for educational leaders-in-training in the art of positive conflict resolution, in developing the ability to "agree and disagree agreeably," and in practicing behaviors that respect the dignity of each participant as they de-escalate conflicts. Academy training in conflict resolution is based on the belief that conflict is necessary for growth, that organizations can succeed even if all members are unable to agree on all topics, and that it is the responsibility of leaders to guide others toward this awareness. Training is focused on developing conversations based on communicating perspectives, understanding the other person's perspective, and working together to resolve conflicts. These conversations often result in learning more about the other person, which can significantly change understanding of the people and the problems involved (Stone, Patton, & Heen, 1999). Learning about conflict resolution models and then being allowed time to apply models within the context of multiple field-based experiences is a natural component of the integrated, spiraling curriculum in partnership academies. And, again, as students reach proficiency, they are involved with and assist in designing increasingly more difficult assignments.

SITUATIONAL AWARENESS

Situational awareness applies to a leader who is "aware of the details and undercurrents in the running of the school and uses this information to address current and potential problems" (Waters, Marzano, & McNulty, 2003, p. 4). This leadership responsibility is often required by both university and school leaders as complex situations develop daily, and it is included in the curriculum and applied throughout the length of the training in partnership academies. Leaders in business also use this responsibility, and a variety of models exist to help new leaders gain competence in situational awareness. Leaders today must take into consideration the unintended consequences of actions and always be alert to ethical dilemmas. This type of awareness, although difficult to teach, can be learned. Heifetz and Linsky (2002) described such awareness as "staying on the balcony and being on the dance floor" at the same time (as cited in Fullan, 2005, p. 103). Fullan further defined "the balcony" as "standing back to get perspective" and the "dance floor" as "the intense leadership for deep learning" (p. 103). This high awareness of surroundings at all levels of the organization was described as "emotional quotient" in *Primal Leadership,* by Goleman, Boyatzis, and McKee (2002), and was included as a strong leadership skill throughout the text. Covey's (1989) fifth habit for effective leaders referred to this same skill: "Seek first to understand, then to be understood" (p. 235). Leaders today without a strong awareness of how people think and a corresponding high level of skill in negotiating with students, staff, parents, and community members will face extreme difficulties. In the partnership academy model, extended, multiple field experiences with the support of an experienced mentor and collaborative university and public school planners give leaders-in-training invaluable practice in developing situational awareness by applying theory to practice, as part of the integrated, spiraling curriculum.

RESILIENCY SKILLS

The demands on administrators are many; the problems are unlimited; the time for rest is limited; and no matter how hard administrators try to please their constituents, some segments of the population will always be unhappy and many problems will remain unresolved. Administrators who are able to thrive despite these realities can strengthen themselves and their organizations by being well acquainted with and applying resiliency research. Habits of mind for themselves and for their stakeholders can be developed that offset the effects of debilitating, constant stress faced today by all these groups. In the partnership academy for leaders model, university and school leaders assist prospective administrators by sharing resources and demonstrating ways to embed system supports within the organization for sustainability of the leaders and of the organization. As is the case with developing conflict resolution skills, the development of resiliency skills in stakeholders results in improving the overall organizational outcomes.

Six ways schools, families, and communities could work together to embed protective factors in their environments to increase resiliency were identified by Henderson (1998): "Increase bonding, set clear and consistent boundaries, teach life skills, provide caring and support, set and communicate high standards, provide opportunities for meaningful participation" (p. 18). Henderson's findings were parallel to those from Werner and Smith's (1982) seminal study, *Vulnerable but Invincible: A Longitudinal Study of Resilient Children and Youth,* and both of these older studies have been upheld and strengthened by current research.

Embedding protective factors within organizations can increase resiliency for both children and adults, and these supports should be a part of all educational systems, including the leadership preparation partnerships. As examples, opportunities can be provided for students and adults to develop bonding relationships. In the case of the academy leadership preparation programs, these relationships occur between cohort members and between students and mentors, but the relationship building also happens as students and planners work together regularly throughout the course of and following the two-year program. An additional benefit is the long-term relationship that develops between university and district planners. Goleman's research (2006) has reinforced the correlation of strong relationships to resiliency.

The leadership preparation partnership approach we are suggesting offers additional ways to embed protective factors within the two-year preparation program: allowing participants to increase their sense of mastery throughout the program as they design their own internships within parameters; allowing them to work within their own settings; and asking them to apply theory and research to their own practices to develop mastery-level skills. The collegiality built within the long-term, frequent interactions builds social competencies, as well as academic skills. The partnership itself and ongoing collaboration of the planners illustrates to students the power of developing a systemwide approach. Preparation for the vision of leadership that we espouse can occur only within a close *collaborative* partnership between the formal preparation program provider (usually a university) and a school district willing to blend current theories and best practices with rich, supervised, field experiences.

REFLECTIVE PRACTICE

An important feature of the integrated, spiraling curriculum is the opportunity to introduce and develop the skill of reflecting. This is one of the most powerful tools for professional growth and development for teachers and another essential component of the spiraling curriculum. Current brain research upholds reflection as an important component for improving individuals and organizations, as stated by York-Barr, Sommers, Ghere, and Montie (2006):

> We believe that now more than ever before, educators must continuously and meaningfully reflect on their practice—by themselves and with their colleagues. . . . We are equally convinced that without significant advances in the capacity of individuals and schools to foster continuous renewal and improvement, the demands on educators will exceed their capacity to promote high levels of learning for all students. (p. xxii)

Reflection involves taking time from the frantic pace of everyday life to think about actions and reactions and determine what lessons were learned, a practice referred to previously as "stepping out on the balcony" for a broader perspective. Reflection is a skill needed by instructors, students, and stakeholders within schools and universities and leadership training. Reflecting requires both critical and creative thinking and often results in questions about practice and theory, followed by the development of new practices and theories or the refinement of current practices and theories. A spiraling, integrated curriculum positions reflection as an automatic activity and part of ongoing field experiences throughout the preparation program. Written reflections are an integral component of the final performance assessment.

Though students may be less than excited about the requirement for frequent reflections early on, most indicate by the end of the program that reflection was a significant contributor to their growth. It is important for prospective leaders to keep chronological journals, to review their growth, have evidence of processing experiences, and have a visible record of the changes in habits of mind they have made over time. Reflection is a continuous, spiraling process. Actions are completed, and reflections are made that result in thoughts and refinements for the next practice, followed by reflection and additional changes in practice—another sample of the integrated, spiraling curriculum and theory-into-practice, practice-into-theory approach.

Reflection required in the partnership academies can be in the form of verbal or written thoughts regarding coursework, readings, and internships and relate back to experiences with instructors, mentors, or fellow students. Through reflection, students gain awareness of the thinking of veteran leaders compared with their own, and they develop skills in questioning and evaluating for use with their own students and communities. Developing the art of questioning is an important skill for today's leaders, as questions need to be asked often about educational mandates, student benefits, and why we continue practices that no longer work. As students work through the spiraling curriculum over a two-year period, their reflections become increasingly more complex, and their questions become more evaluative in nature.

Reflective leaders strengthen organizations by putting reflective systems in place in order to create growth-oriented organizations for learning. Reflection produces renewal and enhancement and defends against stagnation. As all members of the partnership academies become proficient in the art of reflection, an added benefit of increasing the leadership capacity for partner organizations accrues.

Reflection is an integral part of the assessment process for partnership academy programs. The practice of weekly reflections is established through class time set aside for that purpose or through regular electronic communication. Written comments document the thought process and serve as indicators of student progress throughout the program. Students reflect verbally and in writing, individually and in groups, in classes, in their journals, with their mentors, and online. Formal benchmark reflections (end of each semester, first year, second year) allow students to assess their own progress and share their beliefs with mentors and planners. Students' final reflections are part of a performance assessment, which includes past and current reflections to show the stages of their development, along with the real-world evidence of student competencies from their internships.

Mentors take a strong role in guiding leaders-in-training through the reflection practice, sharing their own reflections, asking questions that lead students to higher levels of thinking, and modeling reflection in their own practice. The reflective-practice aspect of the spiraling-curriculum approach allows planners and mentors to make ongoing adjustments based on individual student progress. Finally, reflection is supported by brain research: "The reflective process incorporates an executive function that purposefully accesses, coordinates, and directs the vast resources of the brain in the exercise of complex reasoning" (Dickmann et al., 2004, p. 12).

CREATING INDIVIDUALIZED, SUPERVISED FIELD EXPERIENCES

Field experiences in partnership academies reflect the spiraling curriculum and differentiated instruction approaches and the important blending of the roles of the student, mentor, supervisor, and planners in developing individualized experiences. Planners establish the expectations and parameters for the internships, based on current leadership frameworks, university credit, and district needs. Students need to be clear about their interests, strengths, and needs and share this with their mentors. Immediate supervisors in the district are apprised of the partnership goals and then collaborate with students and mentors in identifying needs that might allow students to develop proficiency in the selected areas, in gradually increasing levels of responsibility. At the beginning of the preparation program, students may be observing leaders and reflecting on current practices compared to the research. Gradually, their leadership responsibilities will increase as they move from minor to major leadership roles.

The differentiated instruction follows as each student has unique experiences. Mutual interests may result in partnering within the student group, but each student must have assigned specific and separate responsibilities. Students are encouraged to use their growing understandings and skills in systems thinking and situational awareness to identify unrecognized needs and develop appropriate solutions. The high-stakes accountability and mounds of data analysis and interpretation needed to meet the No Child Left Behind Act of 2001 (NCLB) requirements provide a wealth of possible experiences for students. Districts that have serious needs and inadequate personnel to meet those needs can identify projects for students to consider, which is another way to strengthen the district and benefit students. In our experience, these district projects have been expanded as students exhibit competence and, often, exceptional leadership skills. Again, the integrated, spiraling curriculum grows in complexity as the program progresses.

Individualized field experiences add another level of increasing understanding and proficiency and allow for students' unique individual talents and needs to be demonstrated. In preparation for developing opportunities for students, district leaders review district needs and goals in order to identify areas for improvement that could be supplemented by internships. University staff will need to review and revise traditional requirements to match the partnership expectations. All planners need to work together on the development of the guidelines, with frequent monitoring of activities and outcomes. There are two strong benefits of this approach. University programs become steeped in both theory and practice, improve the connection to the real world, and strengthen student performance; districts gain a cadre of quality leaders-in-training who are able to develop field experiences that benefit the district and the community.

TRAINING MENTORS FOR FIELD EXPERIENCES

A long-term (over the length of the preparation program) relationship with a mentor adds to the spiraling curriculum and gives it depth. In partnership academies for leaders, mentors are selected carefully. They believe in this new vision of leadership and are able to model it as well as guide prospective leaders in practicing it. These mentors must also be reflective practitioners, skilled in the art of developing a spiraling curriculum that is integrated with students' coursework, work assignments, and abilities. Mentors are given guidance as to the standards and frameworks students will be reviewing, are kept informed of all partnership efforts and activities, and have leeway to guide mentees gradually through the processing of the class curriculum and development of experiences throughout the length of the program. These field experiences are matched to students' individual strengths, interests, and abilities and focus on helping them develop needed skills in areas of improvement over the two-year period. These experiences are also matched with building and district needs, which will help develop student abilities in situational awareness and systems thinking, as well as relate to the overall building and district school improvement plans.

Mentors can be very helpful in processing and evaluating events and outcomes with mentees, sharing their own ideas, and asking probing questions to pull mentees up to ever-increasing levels of performance. Although the mutually nurturing relationships are a strong outcome for the mentees and often last beyond the formal relationship, mentors in partnership academies report personal growth and express appreciation for the opportunity to strengthen their own educational commitments and beliefs and give back to the profession. They often find their own service revitalized and their professional knowledge base updated as a result of the connection to a leader-in-training and the partnership effort and being able to share with others what they have learned. Many choose to further their professional growth as a result of their involvement in these partnerships. Educational leaders are often in isolated positions, and regular involvement with active learners defrays the isolation and results in extended networks for participants and planners, thus increasing the resiliency of both groups. Academy mentees often express gratitude for having very busy current leaders share time and ideas with them as they grow in their own leadership skills. Mentoring is a vital component of the spiraling curriculum—it adds a high level of collegiality and brings passion to the participants.

PERFORMANCE ASSESSMENT

Performance assessment has become increasingly important in the field of education. Many states now require some type of performance assessment and licensure exam for their teachers, and many are adding similar requirements for new administrators. One type of performance assessment, the *portfolio,* is recommended to document university and public school partnership training programs, as well as individual student competencies. Portfolio assessment "is a powerful tool for the assessment of student competencies. . . . This type of analysis can provide vital information regarding the validity and strength of administrative preparation programs" (Miller & Salsberry, 2005, p. 29). Portfolios allow each student to demonstrate unique capabilities, strengths, style, and growth from the beginning of his or her preparation program to the completion of the requirements. As documentation is completed throughout the length of the partnership academy program, completion of the portfolio supplements the integrated, spiraling-curriculum approach, as well as the reflective practices. Students are expected to merge theory and practice in their reflection, citing current research for their practices.

Portfolio expectations are communicated from the beginning of the academy program. Students continuously study, revise, and update artifacts as part of the spiraling curriculum. Students work on compiling evidence throughout the length of the program, and the evidence gradually improves with the increasing degree of participation as a leader. The understanding of leadership and the ability to evaluate and revise (reflect upon) their own performance as a leader also improves the experience. One of the goals of the program is for students to increase the ability to self-assess their own performance.

University and school planners need to work together to determine the expectations that encourage students to build upon research-based leadership frameworks and demonstrate their grasp of leadership theories, their ability to apply those theories to practice, and their ability to document and evaluate their own performance. In partnership academies, planners collaboratively develop a process and rubrics for measuring student performance that aligns with the goals of the partnership and the identified leadership frameworks. Student-led conferences at the end of the first and second years are an important component of this performance assessment, allowing students to verbally share their perceptions, identify their growth and need areas, and describe their roles and lessons learned from leadership internship and mentoring activities. A mentor reflection in the portfolio allows mentors to review students' growth in relationship to the standards. In effect, the portfolio assessment documents the spiraling curriculum as students identify their growth over the length of the preparation program. Partnership academies for leaders require the following components in the portfolio:

- Résumé
- Program of studies
- Belief statement
- Brief descriptions of several leadership experiences during the length of the preparation program. These descriptions should describe the leadership role (what was actually done) as well as the content of the experience
- One artifact for each standard that best showcases competencies. A rationale statement should be included with each of these artifacts
- Copies of the Interstate School Leaders Licensure Consortium (ISLLC) standards for self-assessment from three phases of the leader-in-training program: "pre" (completed during the first course in this program); "mid" (completed at the end of the first four courses), and "post" (completed at the end of the program)
- Reflection statement: an executive summary of professional growth, synthesizing perceptions of growth over time, from the beginning of the program to the end. An identification of strengths and weaknesses and plans for future professional development should be part of this reflection. Students should be encouraged to include references to coursework and/or research
- Reflections on attainment of standards: a definition for each standard and a reflection regarding the acquisition of knowledge (what you know), dispositions (what you believe), and performances (what you can do) as applied to each standard
- Mentor's reflection of growth and competencies

The portfolio is the final assessment for a degree and/or licensure, but the true performance assessment is success in the real world. Our graduates have assumed a varying array of leadership positions in school districts. The networking that evolves over the length of these partnership programs enables both universities and schools to remain connected to their leaders-in-training and informed about their performance and progress after they complete the program.

SUMMARY

The long-term, integrated, spiraling curriculum is a major component of partnership academies for leaders—our approach for revitalizing the relationships between universities and public schools. These partnerships become similar to research and development departments of many corporations. Setting aside specific time for educational leaders and learners to talk about current educational theories and practices results in a renewal for all participants and for their organizations. All of the roles are rotated: Sometimes the learners are the students, and sometimes the learners are the teachers and planners. Sometimes the leaders are the planners, and sometimes the leaders are the students. The mentor-mentee relationships also are reciprocal; many mentors as well as mentees tell us of their growth through the mentoring process. The integrated, spiraling nature of the curriculum allows learners to develop increasing levels of understanding and proficiency in authentic settings and to be more aware of their strengths and needs—and also aware of those of the planners and mentors—through reflection and final documentation of the performance assessment.

Each element mentioned in this chapter demonstrates reasons we have moved from a traditional curriculum design for preparing school leaders to a collaborative partnership design with individualized, supervised field experiences. The integrated, spiraling-curriculum approach supports a dynamic, growth-oriented training program that is based in research and articulated in practice in the real world. Leaders trained through this model are better prepared for the world they face upon completion of their programs because they were trained in that world in real time. They are steeped in theory, research, and practice. And they have developed their own projects, at their own pace. The networking that results from the class sessions, the field experiences, and the mentoring provides participants with a rich support system from which to work—a support system that has been lacking in traditional preparation programs—one that reduces the isolation often mentioned by new educational leaders as a reason to leave the profession entirely.

6

Developing Ethical Leaders

To educate a person in mind and not in morals is to educate a menace to society.

—President Theodore Roosevelt

Ethics is about good and evil, right and wrong, justice and injustice, in individuals and in our relationships to people and organizations. This chapter rests on the assumption that leadership is a subset of ethics rather than ethics being a subset of leadership. It examines the ethics of what leaders are, what they do, and how they do it. It aims at expanding the reader's ethical point of view by first considering personal ethics, then moving on to look at leadership and the common good.

Educational leaders shape the ethical environment of their schools and districts. Effective educational leaders must be able to reflect on the ethical dimensions of power and leadership. The primary purpose of this chapter is to clarify the ethical responsibilities of educational leaders. However, it must also be noted that whenever two or more organizations embark on a joint venture, there are ethical dimensions that must be considered. As new partnerships emerge, there will be ethical dilemmas that must be faced.

For example, some professors have been reluctant to engage in cooperative delivery activities because they believe that such cooperation is an encroachment upon their turf. Historically, professors have decided what they would teach and when their courses would be offered. They then expected students to come to campus and enroll in these courses. Consequently, some resisted efforts to involve school districts in "their area." Similarly, some school leaders have believed that "ivory tower" professors were out of touch with the current school environment. Some are suspicious about spending valuable time discussing "leadership theory."

Traditions often survive long after the original reason for them no longer exists. Aristotle said that organizations are created to meet times and situations, and they must be fluid. As the needs of the educational profession change, universities and school districts must be able to modify and adjust themselves and their organizations to meet this new situation. A failure to perceive change and accommodate it can result in a dysfunctional system. However, any attempt to change existing relationships has the potential of triggering resistance. It is impossible to have change without stress, and most people react to stress by either fighting against the perceived threat or avoiding the threat. This chapter helps both professors and practicing administrators identify ethical conflicts and offers strategies for resolving these conflicts.

ETHICAL DECISION MAKING

Effective educational leaders are much more than the sum of what they know and what they can do. With the acceleration of change, knowledge and skills are largely transitory. Character, in contrast, is enduring. As we strive to develop and prepare better educational leaders, we must ask ourselves two fundamental questions: "What are our ethical standards?" and "How do we apply these standards in educational leadership situations?"

Educational leaders need a process or model to help them make sense of the ethical issues they face. The purpose of this section is to offer a schema that allows educational leaders to incorporate ethical decision making into their day-to-day experiences. The goal of an ethical leader should be to promote justice and the common good—work has become increasingly important as we face the unintended consequences of our current high-stakes accountability for ourselves and for our students.

Ethics poses questions not only about how we ought to lead but also according to what standards leadership decisions are right or wrong. Discussing ethics forces us to identify character traits necessary to be effective leaders. Although any discussion of ethics includes thoughts about values, religion, and the law, being ethical is not just a matter of following feelings. Nor is ethics confined to religious beliefs. And although the law often incorporates ethics, there are many examples of laws that are challenged as being unethical.

Although the vast majority of educators are competent, capable, caring people, some are not. The front pages of daily newspapers make it clear that some educators make decisions that are dishonest, wrongheaded, and unethical. The question is "What can be done to improve the quality of educational decision making?" The place to start changing is with each of us taking responsibility for our own behavior and holding those who work with children to a higher standard of ethical behavior. Incorporating ethics into leadership preparation programs is critical to improving the quality of educational decision making.

WHY PEOPLE MAKE BAD CHOICES

Four rationalizations are used to justify questionable conduct: (1) believing that the activity is not "really" illegal or immoral, (2) believing that the action is in the individual's or the organization's best interests, (3) believing that the action will never be found out, and (4) believing that because the action helps the organization, the organization should condone it (Gellerman, 1986).

Those who use the first rationalization depend on a very narrow view of rules to guide their decisions. They believe that if something is not specifically prohibited or if there is some ambiguity in the interpretation of the rule, they are free to do whatever they want. School districts that do not have a comprehensive ethical code of conduct, or do not explicitly state that no decision will be tolerated that violates this ethical code, facilitate rationalization. Educational leaders who give the impression that they do not care about means, but only ends, tacitly encourage their subordinates to make unethical decisions. People who are put into ambiguous, ill-defined situations can easily cross over the boundary separating the ethical from the unethical. Principals who know that some teachers give unearned grades to athletes, and coaches who allow injured star student athletes to decide whether they are able to play are examples of people using this first rationalization.

Those who use the second rationalization, self-interest, seem to believe that the individual's or organization's best interests are the only considerations that matter. These people look only at results and are not concerned about how those results are obtained. Educational leaders reinforce this attitude when they overlook "minor" ethical indiscretions or give only token punishment to breaches of ethics. A school district that encourages certain students or groups of students to be absent from school on testing day and a curriculum director who accepts special benefits from a book publisher for adopting a certain book series are examples of educators with poorly developed ethical compasses. Today's high-stakes-accountability environment increases the potential for this type of rationalization.

The third rationalization for making unethical choices is the belief that it is unethical only if you get caught. This type of person has no personal moral compass and believes that if the unethical behavior is undetected, it is not unethical. There is evidence that an increasing number of college students hold this belief. It is not uncommon for them to say, "It isn't cheating if you don't get caught." It is likely that the generation of educational leaders will be increasingly younger as the "baby boomer" population retires. Again, the teaching of ethics becomes even more important for leaders-in-training, as well as leaders in practice.

The fourth rationalization is not based upon a lack of clarity about what is unethical. Rather, it is based on the belief that whatever the school board or educational leader says is correct is therefore ethical. For example, if the district policy prevents parents from requesting a particular teacher for their children but exceptions are made for the children of district employees, it is clear that there are no ethical codes, but only behaviors of convenience. Increasingly, schools are being taken to task for discriminating against groups of students, in not providing a suitable education for *all* students, regardless of need or ability.

ETHICAL SELF-DECEPTION

Self-deception is being unaware of the process that leads to making judgments. Some psychological forces promote ethical self-deception (Tenbrunsel & Messick, 2004). These researchers and others believe it is self-deception that allows individuals to behave according to what is in their own best interests, while at the same time believing that they are upholding high moral principles. When one continually engages in this self-deception, ethics fade into the background and the moral implications of actions are obscured. The four factors that enable a person to engage in self-deception are language euphemisms, the slippery slope of decision making, errors in perceptual causation, and constraints induced by representations of the self (Tenbrunsel & Messick, 2004, p. 223).

Using *language euphemisms* is the process of selecting words that disguise unethical actions. By renaming actions, we may be able to accept actions that when viewed objectively are unacceptable. The function of this practice is to make self-interest behaviors seem more benign. For example, when discussing the reporting process of the No Child Left Behind Act, it sounds less racist to say, "We are excluding test scores of any group of students deemed too small to be statistically significant" than to say, "The scores of minority students in our school district are not reported by racial category." To say, "A teacher was asked to leave the district because he demonstrated poor judgment by engaging in an inappropriate relationship with a student" sounds much better than saying, "One of our teachers was fired because he molested a student." Language euphemisms are not simply deceptive and misleading; they are unethical. Using language euphemisms causes us to fool ourselves, and also attempts to fool others, into believing that our actions do not have an ethical impact.

The second enabler of self-deception is *the slippery slope of decision making*. This is the numbing effect of engaging in the same activity over and over. The discomfort that the initial unethical act caused gradually reduces until the ethical temptation or dilemma is no longer recognized. After a period of time, the repetition of the unethical act normalizes actions until the act no longer seems unethical. For example, an educational leader who routinely inflates her supply budget by 20% may eventually convince herself that that this behavior is the standard practice and is, therefore, an acceptable behavior.

Errors in perceptual causation is the third enabler of self-deception. This is the tendency to assign blame not on an objective evaluation, but by our preconceived perceptions. For example, there are many documented cases of school leaders failing to see the signs that a teacher was sexually abusing a child when the teacher was otherwise an exemplary teacher. If, in addition, the educational leader personally likes the teacher, if the teacher has superior teaching ratings, and if the teacher seems to be well liked, the educational leader is more likely to overlook threshold behaviors that might be signs of abuse. This tendency is increased if the complaining child has previously been in trouble. Furthermore, principals may deceive themselves and not see what is actually happening, especially in cases in which the principal identifies with the suspect teacher. Some individuals deceive themselves into thinking that they see the world objectively. This phenomenon is known as "constraints induced by representations of self." This means that it is impossible for anyone to have a truly objective perception of the effects of his or her actions on others (Tenbrunsel & Messick, 2004). This failure to understand how we are perceived leads to making unethical decisions, because we do not understand our role in various interactions. For example, a principal who tells her staff, "My daughter is selling Girl Scout cookies, but don't feel that you have to buy any," may actually believe that all of her teachers actually wanted to buy six boxes of cookies. This principal failed to understand the power differential and, consequently, unethically used her position to force teachers to engage in an activity in which many of them would not have willingly participated without her undue pressure.

The first step toward reducing the likelihood of ethical self-deception is to recognize and accept it as a real problem. The next step is to be on alert for signs that we are engaging in self-deception, and rethink our actions (Tenbrunsel & Messick, 2004).

ETHICAL BEHAVIOR

While students are in school, they are influenced by the academic curriculum and the curriculum of helping students learn how to be happy, productive citizens. Parents send their children to school expecting it to be a safe, orderly, fair environment in which their children will be respected. Students are very adept at noticing inconsistencies between what educators say and what they do. Because there are not enough police or regulation agencies to uncover every violation of accepted behavior, society must depend upon the voluntary acceptance of standards of ethics. Educators have long been expected to be exemplars for their students and held to a higher standard of behavior than the general public.

Although there are obviously some people who should never have been allowed into education, most educators are good people. However, without strong ethical values, school districts and school employees can easily drift from proper to questionable to illegal behaviors resulting in costly criminal and civil litigation. It is not uncommon for individuals when accused or arrested to assert that they "never meant to violate the law." In retrospect, they often admit they gradually began to do more and more things that led them down the path toward illegal action. When confronted with an allegation of unethical behavior, these people often sincerely profess that they "did not mean any harm."

Regulations are generally not enacted until after an unacceptable behavior has occurred. There is no need for rules to regulate behavior that is accepted as ethical by the majority of society. Only when society perceives an increase in unethical behavior are laws and regulations made to control the unwanted behavior. For example, prior to the Columbine, Colorado, school shooting, in 1999, few school districts saw a need to have a policy prohibiting bringing guns to school.

Once an educator or school district is viewed as immoral or unethical, it is incredibly difficult to regain the public's trust. Highly respected individuals who choose immoral or unethical behaviors will likely never be viewed as ethical again. Society rarely forgets and is slow to forgive unethical behavior.

Teachers teach best and students learn best in an open, creative, ethical environment. Educational leaders who are seen as being unfair have difficulty attracting and retaining the highest-quality teachers. Community members will take pride in the accomplishments of their schools only if they believe that the people who work there do not bend rules, cut corners, or hurt people.

PSYCHOLOGICAL COMPONENTS OF ETHICAL LEADERSHIP

Ethics is at the heart of leadership. A culture's ethical values define the concept of leadership (Ciulla, 1995). Badly led organizations will wind up doing unethical things. Educational leaders are responsible for the ethical environment of their school districts or schools. Consequently, a major task for educational leaders is to bring colleagues together around common values.

Ethical fitness is like physical fitness—it has to be practiced. The four psychological components of ethical behavior are moral sensitivity, moral judgment, moral motivation, and moral character (Rest & Narvaez, 1994).

Moral sensitivity refers to awareness of how our actions affect other people. It can be summed up in the concept that intent is irrelevant; the impact of one's actions determines one's level of moral sensitivity. An example that may seem trivial at first glance is the controversy that continues in many communities regarding the use of mascots, specifically the "Indian" as the mascot for athletic teams. For years, Native American groups and others have pleaded with school officials to change this practice, arguing that using a people as a mascot demeans them and causes them serious pain. In debates held in communities across the country, some speakers have openly wept as they described why this practice is hurtful and disrespectful. Many defenders of the status quo have replied that they do not intend any harm. In fact, they often say they are honoring Native Americans by using this mascot, believing that these protesters should just "get over it." This attitude is an example of moral insensitivity.

Moral judgment involves the process of deciding what is right and wrong in a specific situation. A *moral temptation* occurs when we know that something is unethical, but we want to do it anyway. A *moral dilemma* occurs when we are confronted by a decision in which both options are congruent with our values. Often, these dilemmas are between justice versus mercy, truth versus loyalty, short term versus long term, or individual versus community (Kidder, 1995).

For example, a school policy states that no student may take part in any interscholastic sport if he or she drinks alcohol. A coach smells the odor of alcohol on the breath of a student athlete. She knows the youngster has been drinking, but the athlete is a star on the team and "basically a good kid." Should the educator turn the youngster in or look the other way and hope that the youngster will not again violate the school policy? The process of deciding what to do in this scenario is an example of using moral judgment.

Moral motivation refers to the importance given to moral values that may be in competition with other values. For example, one of your school's most generous supporters might refuse to contribute as long as he has to interact with a certain new employee, and he asks to interact with someone else. Would it matter if the new employee were a person of color, or a woman, or gay? How difficult would it be to reject the booster's request? It is easy to make moral decisions in the abstract. However, only when there is some type of price to be paid for the actions do you know your moral motivation.

Moral character refers to the practice of ethical leadership. People generally follow a predictable pattern of four stages when forming their values. The first is an internal acceptance of a value; next, comes a public statement of that value; an action follows that exhibits the value; and, finally, there is a repeated consistent action in accordance with the value. It is quite easy to think of oneself as an ethical person. However, until consistently acted upon, this value has not been adopted. This is why codes of ethics are so important to school districts. In these codes, the values of the school district are made public. Once codes are made public, the district can expect employees to conform to the values and can hold the district accountable to its code of ethics. Of course, no educational leader is perfect. There will be times when individuals will not live up to their ethical codes. However, a conscious effort to do so is a sign of moral character. When all is said and done, a leader is either trusted or is not. Only when others can predict what values underlie our actions do we know what these values are. For many, the best predictor of what a person will do is what he or she just did.

Ethical decision making is a skill that takes practice. Would you want to explain the reasons for all of your decisions to your students? Kidder (1995) sees this as a question of ethical fitness. Just as physical fitness requires constant effort, moral fitness requires a conscious effort to make moral decisions. Bernard Bass, in his 1997 article, "The Ethics of Transformational Leadership," stated that leaders become transformational only when they increase their awareness of what is right, good, and important and they assist their colleagues in moving from acting in their self-interests to acting for the good of their school communities.

THEORIES AND STAGES OF ETHICAL DEVELOPMENT

Two main theorists on moral development are commonly recognized: Kohlberg and Gilligan. Components of their theories are reviewed in this section.

Kohlberg's Theory of Moral Development

Kohlberg (1984) believed that as people gain more cognitive ability with age, they are able to move to a higher stage. His theory of moral reasoning is a *stage theory,* meaning that each stage must be sequential and no stage can be skipped. However, not everyone automatically moves from one stage to the next as they mature. Kohlberg believed that movement from one stage to another occurs only when a person notices inadequacies in his or her present way of coping with a given moral dilemma. According to this theory, individuals can understand moral reasoning only one stage ahead of where they are. For example, a person in Stage 2 can understand Stage 3 reasoning, but nothing beyond that.

Stage 1 of moral thinking is generally found in children of elementary school age. Adults at this stage do not really understand the rules of a society. At this stage,

> physical consequences of an action determine its goodness or badness regardless of the human meaning or value of these consequences. Avoidance of punishment and unquestioning deference to power are valued in their own right, not in terms of respect for an underlying moral order supported by punishment and authority. (Duska & Whelen, 1975, pp. 45–46)

At this stage, decisions are made on the basis of a concern for the self: "I should not do this, because I might get in trouble." At this stage, people are primarily concerned with avoiding punishment. They do what people in authority tell them to do. For example, a person at this stage might reason that she should not falsify her résumé because if she gets caught, she might lose her job. In the "Heinz dilemma" (a well-known example used in discussions of ethics and morality), Heinz must decide whether or not to steal a drug that would save his wife's life. Some might say that Heinz should not steal the drug because he might get caught and go to jail. Conversely, a person at this stage might say that Heinz should steal the drug because if he does not, his family will be displeased with him.

At Stage 2, people are still at an egocentric stage. However, actions are now judged as correct if they satisfy one's needs or involve a "fair exchange." The concept of reciprocity plays a big part in the decisions of a person at this stage. People at this stage are not interested in what is right; they do what they think is in their best interests. For example, an athletic director's willingness to permit a coach to play an injured athlete may feel justified on the grounds that "I know it is wrong, but this is the championship game. And besides, we would have probably won anyway, and the student might earn a college scholarship." According to Kohlberg, for people at Stage 2, a correct action is one "which instrumentally satisfies one's own needs and occasionally the needs of others" (Duska & Whelen, 1975, p. 46). Simply stated, *reciprocity* means "If you scratch my back, I'll scratch yours."

People in Stage 3 are motivated by a strong desire for approval, the primary motivator for actions at this stage. Will the superintendent approve of this action? At this stage, intention becomes important for the first time. For example, she made a bad decision, but her "heart was in the right place" (Duska & Whelen, 1975).

For people at Stage 4, conforming to the rules is very important. Most decisions are based upon knowing and then following the rules. Law and order is of utmost importance. These people believe that deviating from the rules will result in unbounded chaos. For example, in a school setting, the strict observation of the law would require a principal to discipline a teacher who was late to school because of the illness of his child. Right behavior consists of doing one's duty, showing respect for authority, and maintaining the given social order for its own sake.

People at Stage 5 try to do the "right thing," regardless of the rules. They no longer strictly conform to rules and regulations. They work to replace rules that do not protect the rights of individuals or of society. At this stage, right action tends to be defined in terms of general individual rights and in terms of standards that have been critically examined and agreed upon by the whole society.

At Stage 6, a person has developed a conscious sense of personal ethics. These people have strong standards of ethical decision making regardless of individual situations. All individual acts are judged as right or wrong on the basis of these categorical imperatives. An example of a categorical imperative is "Do unto others as you would have them do unto you." According to Kohlberg,

> Right is defined by the decision of conscience in accord with self-chosen ethical principles appealing to logical comprehensiveness, universality and consistency. These are universal principles of justice, of the reciprocity and equality of human rights, and of respect for the dignity of human beings as individual persons. (Kohlberg & Hersh, 1977, p. 54)

While Kohlberg believed in the existence of Stage 6, he did not believe that everyone reaches this stage. He was more concerned with the process of making moral decisions than with the individual decision that a person would make. Although moral reasoning does not ensure moral action, making a conscious decision to accept a moral code will likely ensure that your motivation will be generally driven by this code.

Gilligan's Theory

Gilligan criticized Kohlberg's theory because the study included only privileged White males and because his theory considered male views of individual rights and rules as being higher than women's points of view on development, in terms of their caring effect on human development. She asserted that women and men have differing moral and psychological tendencies. And since men have dominated the discussion of moral theory, women's perspectives are often not taken seriously and are not considered as developed or sophisticated (Gilligan, 1982). She concluded that women think in terms of caring and relationships and men think in terms of rules and justice. Gilligan encouraged society to value both equally. She asserted that women are not inferior in their personal or moral development, but that they are different. They develop in a way that focuses on connections among people (rather than separation) and with an ethic of care for people (rather than an ethic of justice). According to Gilligan's theory, the male approach to morality is that individuals have certain basic rights and that rights of others must be respected. So, morality imposes restrictions on what someone can do. She believed that females approach morality from the point of view that that people have responsibilities toward others. Gilligan (1982) summarized this by saying that male morality has a "justice orientation" and that female morality has a "responsibility orientation."

CLASSIFYING ETHICAL THEORIES

The study of ethics generally involves organizing values, deciding on beliefs, and recommending standards of right and wrong behavior. Three strategies for applying ethics to real situations are duty theories, consequentialist theories, and virtue theories.

Duty Theory

Duty, or rule-based, theories base morality on the concept of obligation. The consequences of an action are not considered when making decisions. For example, Kant argued that there are certain self-evident principles of reason, which he called "categorical imperatives." According to Kant, it does not matter what an individual wants to do. Kant's most famous categorical imperative is "treat people as an end, never as a means to an end" (as cited in Paton, 1971, pp. 165–178). Kant believed that individuals intuitively know their duty.

Consequentialist Theory

The basic premise of consequentialist theory is that an action is right if the consequences of the action are more favorable than unfavorable for most people. These people are ends based rather than rule based. Before acting, they calculate the good and bad impact of an action. The end result of the action is the only determining factor in morality. *Utilitarianism* is a form of consequentialist theory: An action is morally right if the consequences of the action are more favorable than unfavorable.

Virtue Theory

People who base their ethical decision making on virtue, or care-based, theory believe that a person should learn good habits of character by learning and following a group of set rules, such as "Don't kill" and "Don't steal." Virtue theory traces its roots from Plato's emphasis on the four cardinal virtues of wisdom, courage, temperance, and justice. Other virtues that might be included in a value-driven person are honesty, fairness, and faithfulness. The virtue approach to ethics is based upon the belief that there are certain ideals toward which we should strive. With repetition, virtues once acquired become ingrained in the character of a person. According to this theory, a virtuous person is an ethical person.

ETHICAL DILEMMA VERSUS ETHICAL TEMPTATION

Kidder (1995) made the distinction between an ethical temptation and an ethical dilemma. An *ethical temptation* is a right-versus-wrong decision. Everyone faces right-versus-wrong decisions every day. Examples of ethical temptations include falsifying test scores, denying a legitimate request for special education services, or using a school computer to view pornography. In these decisions, the person clearly understands what should be done. However, a more difficult decision occurs between two options that seem to suggest two "right" choices, such that an individual has difficulty identifying either choice as clearly wrong—but both options cannot be chosen. Such decisions are *ethical dilemmas.* When tempted to do what we know is wrong, most of us will resist the temptation and do what is right. However, ethical dilemmas are much more difficult to resolve. School leaders face these types of decisions every day. Kidder identified four patterns of such dilemmas: truth versus loyalty, individual versus community, short term versus long term, and justice versus mercy. Examples of these patterns are presented as scenarios.

Truth Versus Loyalty

A consultant conducted an inservice on sexual harassment and sexual abuse prevention for all of the school staff. At the end of the training, each participant was required to sign a document that affirmed that they attended the training, received a copy of the district policy, and read and understood the policy. On the way back to her classroom, a teacher saw one of her colleagues, a nontenured teacher, arrive late at school after visiting her terminally ill husband at the hospital. She then observed her friend take a form from the table and sign that she had attended the workshop. Turning in her friend could result in the teacher not being offered a contract for next year. Not turning her in might expose a child to being harmed and the district being sued. Whichever course of action she chose would be "right." And she could not choose both.

Individual Versus Community

Sara was a member of a search committee for a new principal. The district policy clearly stated that all committee discussions were to be kept strictly confidential. In addition, the district could be exposed to legal action if the hiring process were not completely fair. During the course of the discussion about the candidates, one of the committee members made a statement that clearly indicated prejudice against women holding supervisory positions. This committee member believed that high school principals should be males. At the conclusion of the process, a male was hired. Sara believed that there was a female candidate clearly superior to the person that was hired. She knew that if she spoke about the committee's deliberation, her school district might suffer significant economic loss. However, she believed that the unsuccessful candidate was illegally discriminated against. Whichever course of action she chose would be "right." And she could not choose both.

Short Term Versus Long Term

Scott had earned his building license and was ready to take his first principalship. He and his spouse had a five-year old child. His partner was responsible for most of the child care while Scott was in school, but Scott promised that when he finished graduate school, he would more equally share the family responsibilities. The superintendent told Scott that he was on track to get the next principalship that opened up. However, the superintendent suggested that in order to strengthen his position, Scott should take on more district committee responsibilities and assist with district teacher recruitment. Scott knew that when he became a principal, it would mean financial security for his family. However, the superintendent's recommendation also meant that he would have to increase the hours he spent at work and throw most of the family responsibilities onto his spouse. He would not able to play ball with his child, nor would he be there to help his son with his schoolwork. Whichever course of action he chose would be "right." And he could not choose both.

Justice Versus Mercy

A principal announced that he would be making a special classroom visitation to decide whom to nominate for a sought-after teaching award. Three teachers were finalists for the honor. While observing his favorite teacher, it became obvious that she was having a bad day. She asked whether she could have another visit. The principal knew that the teacher was not getting a chance to demonstrate her competency. However, he also knew that the other two teachers had only one chance to demonstrate their abilities. Whichever course of action he chose would be "right." And he could not choose both.

The above dilemmas are tough choices. They all pit one powerful right against another. Kidder (1995) asserted that to survive, each person needs to develop the capacity to recognize the nature of moral challenges and respond with a well-tuned conscience. Competent educational leaders must clearly understand their own value systems, gather the facts pertaining to the specific dilemma, reason it through, grapple with the tough issues, and make their decisions. Leaders and leaders-in-training must not wait until faced with a dilemma to begin the process of learning how to make ethical decisions. The curriculum for preparing leaders must include ethics.

A FRAMEWORK FOR ETHICAL DECISION MAKING

Competent educational leaders must ask themselves, "According to what standards will I evaluate an action as right or wrong?" The following six steps are offered in partnership academies for leaders as a guide for making ethical decisions:

1. Recognize when you are facing a moral issue.
2. Get the facts before you make any decision.
3. Clarify what individuals and groups have an important stake in the outcome.
4. Review all options for action.
5. Evaluate the impact of the proposed action on all others.
6. Decide which option is the right thing to do.
7. Reflect on the consequences of your decision.

SUMMARY

In partnership academies, educational leaders need to devote a great deal of time to guiding students in developing and understanding their own codes of ethics and possible scenarios that they might face. The theory-into-practice, practice-into-theory approach with an integrated, spiraling curriculum and individualized, field-based internships allows students many opportunities to process and evaluate temptations and dilemmas faced during the term of the training program. Processing is done early and often. These conversations help program leaders, mentors, and leaders-in-training clarify and cement their beliefs and their own codes of ethics. This chapter includes references to many resources used in partnership academies to develop ethical leaders.

7

The PALA Story

An Example of a Partnership Academy for Leaders

In my first year of school administration, I do not think I have been exposed to anything that we didn't discuss at one time or another in PALA. Seriously, I can't imagine where I would be with our school improvement efforts and staff development planning had it not been for the knowledge we received in PALA.

—Academy participant (Gustafson, 2005)

Previous chapters in this book have looked at why we need a new vision for school leadership and introduced general features of partnership academies for leaders, our model for better preparing those leaders. We have explored the advantages of partnerships between universities who prepare leaders and the school districts where they will be employed. We hope we have described the many benefits we have personally observed in these efforts, so that if you are a professor working in

Material from Gustafson, D. M. (2005). *A Case Study of a Professional Administrative Leadership Academy*. Unpublished doctoral dissertation, Kansas State University, Manhattan. Used with permission.

higher education with leaders-in-training, you might find cause for reflection on the ideas presented. If you are a superintendent, we hope you consider the benefits that a collaborative partnership might have in your own environment. If you are a principal, we hope you are thinking about how you might contribute—and benefit from—a professional development program like this. If you are an aspiring leader, we hope this information might stimulate you to explore program options that offer the best preparation for you as an educational leader.

To further describe the partnership concept, this chapter recounts the story of a real partnership between a school district and a large nearby university offering accredited building and district leadership programs. The players are real; the names have been changed. The presentation appears as a single event, but one district partnered with the university on three separate projects over a period of six years. This telling combines what was learned from the three experiences in order to present the best possible example of a working model. In the real world, we believe this model would be of great interest to all four of the critical players introduced in Chapter 1: the professor, the superintendent, the principal, and the leader-in-training. From each perspective, the partnership academy for leaders is a viable resolution of the concerns expressed in those scenarios. We have been in each of these roles ourselves and have experienced firsthand the power of such partnerships.

It is important to note, however, that this chapter is not a "recipe" for others to follow. Each partner and partnership is unique and will have its own story, depending on the situation, the priorities, and the resources available to all parties involved. Partnerships may take many forms; this is an example of one. It is hoped that this chapter will stimulate conversations and actions helpful to those interested in preparing the best school leaders possible, leaders who can thrive in our current high-stakes-accountability environment. This chapter and the "Resources" section will detail the background that led to this academy, the planning process, the establishment of the program framework, the selection process, the identification of partner responsibilities, the mentoring component, the content, the assessment process, the field experiences, the celebrations, and a postscript on the experience.

THE PROFESSIONAL ADMINISTRATIVE LEADERSHIP ACADEMY

A Story of a Collaborative Partnership

Background Information

Jordanville, Silverton, and Morrisburg were three neighboring school districts in the central portion of a midwestern state. They had much in common: similar enrollment, generally similar fiscal resource limits (as a result of state equalization formulas for schools), communities that generally supported their schools, and locations near a major interstate highway. The three districts competed as members of the same athletic league, were long-time rivals, and sometimes competed within the state for resources and recognition. One of the districts included a major state university; one had a visibly more diverse and mobile population with a less stable economy; and one was the home of a major manufacturing plant and other industrial operations.

Despite their differences, the districts had similar problems, and the superintendents of each had great respect for the professional accomplishments of the other two. They frequently sought each other out at state meetings to discuss current topics of mutual interest. On one such occasion, the three were commiserating over the declining number of well-qualified applicants available for recent administrative position openings. All three were concerned that the pool of candidates would continue to shrink in number and in professional competency. The superintendents had worked with leaders from the university located within the boundaries of one of the districts and had shared their frustrations with members of the department of educational administration. Conversations led to convening a meeting of the three district leaders and leaders from the educational administration department at the university to explore what might be done to address this problem.

Those present at the meeting were the three superintendents, the department chair, and another university staff member with partnership experience in another state. The dean of the college of education was unable to attend, but sent his support for the group's efforts. By the close of the first meeting, the superintendents knew if they worked together and partnered with the university, options to address their concerns could be identified. It was spring, and this was the beginning of what was to become the Professional Administrative Leadership Academy (PALA) many months later.

The account that follows is written from the perspective of the Jordanville district and describes the option these partners identified and implemented together to address a concern each had encountered. [Note to readers: One of the authors was actually one of the superintendents in this account, another was a principal mentor, and the third participated as a university instructor.]

The Planning Process

Shortly after the first meeting, the three superintendents were ready to involve other staff members in planning. Selecting the right staff to share in the planning was important. Planners needed to be open to change, believe in the power of collaboration, and have a good understanding of group dynamics—forming, norming, storming, and performing—in case relationships became tenuous as the group worked to find consensus on expectations, requirements, curriculum, instruction, and assessment. When the PALA Planning Committee (PC) was established, it included staff members from each of the three districts with expertise in curriculum, instruction, and staff development design; the two university representatives; and the three superintendents. The superintendents and the department chair believed it was important for them to remain directly involved in the planning and implementation of the academy, since it was to be a dramatic departure from the traditional delivery model in place at the university and from other accredited preparation programs in the area. All members of the educational administration department at the university were invited to attend planning sessions to learn more about the vision for the academy.

The planners in our story spent more than six months preparing their partnership program before the first session was held with participants. In the first month, they decided to initiate a two-year degree program targeting prospective principal candidates from current staff members in each respective district. This program would focus on skills successful school leaders used, and it would be rich in field-based experiences. Participants completing this program would earn a master's degree in educational administration from the university partner and would be eligible for the state license principals were required to hold. They would be well-qualified candidates for future leadership openings in their respective districts. The next step in planning was to determine how to turn this idea into a workable event. The department chair would explore changes necessary in the university practices. The PC was charged to continue to guide, assess, and revise the new program until its completion. The group continued to meet regularly and played a leading role in shaping the academy program throughout its two-year duration. Gustafson (2005) quoted from a taped interview with a PALA planner, showing the interest these leaders brought to the partnership opportunity:

> It became evident to me long ago we were not getting quality candidates in for our school leadership positions, so I thought, we better develop our own, and there is no one better for them to learn from than our own superintendent and building principals. (p. 92)

Establishment of the Program Framework

One of the first decisions facing the PC was selecting the foundation for the preparation program—the framework upon which all of the other components would rest. When choosing a framework, the planners kept in mind the standards that undergird university programs for leadership preparation, such as accreditation requirements and other applicable compliance measures. They also considered current initiatives and priorities in the three districts. The three superintendents established early on that leading the continuous school improvement process was a top priority.

It was agreed that this would be the central theme, the context in which academy content would be delivered. (This was similar to the way magnet schools present curriculum standards in the context of a designated special interest area.)

The framework selected for the PALA was a combination of (1) the *Standards for School Leaders,* which have now been accepted by several states in the United States for licensure and were developed by the Interstate Leadership Licensure Consortium (ISLLC, 1996), and (2) McREL's "21 Leadership Responsibilities" (Waters, Marzano, & McNulty, 2003), which are research based and linked to improved student performance. Planners also looked at the 21 competencies or domains of knowledge and skills identified by the National Policy Board for Educational Administration (NPBEA), a group sponsored by a consortium of professional organizations of educators for the purpose of identifying the core understandings and capabilities required of successful principals.

The next planning task was to decide how to combine these framework pieces. Each of the six ISLLC standards included a list of specific knowledge, dispositions, and performances related to that leadership area. The planners recognized that all 21 McREL responsibilities and the 21 NPBEA competencies could be incorporated in any of the six standards, but they also believed it would be helpful for participants and for those working with them to have a plan for making the connections. The PC developed a matrix showing the interactions between the six standards and the 21 McREL responsibilities and a similar matrix for the standards and the 21 NPBEA competencies.

A brief description of all six ISLLC standards as well as the ISLLC standards format showing knowledge, dispositions, and performances for "Standard I: Vision" appear in Resource A, "ISLLC Standards Summary and Sample." For a similar delineation for the remaining five ISLLC standards, see http://www.ccsso.org/content/pdfs/isllcstd.pdf. A list of "McREL's 21 Responsibilities of School Leaders" (Resource B), the "Matrix Combining ISLLC Standards and McREL's 21 Responsibilities" (Resource C), and the "Matrix Combining ISLLC Standards and NPBEA 21 Competencies" (Resource D) are also included in the "Resources" section.

With the academy framework in place, the planners were ready to set priorities. They realized a key measure of a viable curriculum in any setting is adequate time to deliver it. While they believed all six standards were important, the planners wanted to be sure adequate time was spent on the academy theme: leading continuous school improvement. They would not give all standards equal attention in the academy. The following priorities were established:

- Standard II (culture and instruction) would receive twice as much emphasis as any other standard.
- Standards V (ethics) and Standard VI (the larger context) would receive half as much emphasis as Standard I (vision), Standard III (operations), and Standard IV (collaboration).

This apportionment of time did not reflect on the value of the standards; it was an effort to determine which would make the greatest contribution to leadership in the partner districts at that time. Planners also considered the results of professional development efforts under way in the districts already.

The planners then narrowed the academy focus further by identifying certain performance skills and certain experiences in the school improvement process they regarded as essential to the culture and initiatives under way in each of the districts. University staff coordinating the academy program would make proficiency in these areas a goal for all academy participants. The planners designed two tools to assist them in identifying which knowledge, dispositions, and performances within each of the six standards were most important to the theme of leading school improvement. The first tool ("Importance/Urgency Organizer," Resource E) forced planners to rank items by importance and urgency. The second tool ("Planning Framework by ISLLC Standard," Resource F) helped them brainstorm specific topics and activities for inclusion in the academy program.

With priorities in place, planners began to consider materials needed for the academy. They looked for materials that would increase participants' knowledge in specific areas related to the academy theme and district priorities, such as designing and implementing school improvement plans, addressing achievement gaps, analyzing demographic changes, data analysis and interpretation, and so on. University staff added resources that were effective for introducing related theory and research-based best practice. Web-based materials were located that would be helpful and could facilitate the use of technology throughout the academy. Guided Google searches were also considered as resources.

The Selection Process

Although work on the program content was not yet complete, the PC turned its attention to designing an application and selection process. The planners agreed that the academy would have slots for 24 participants, divided equally among the three district partners. Each district determined its own procedures for selecting the final 8 local participants, but the planners decided there should be a uniform application form, consistent requirements for eligibility to file an application, and a common timeline for selection across all three locations. The university partner agreed to serve as an advisor in the selection process but to leave final determination with the district as long as an applicant met the university's graduate school requirements. It was further agreed that the application process would require each applicant to take the "SRI Perceiver," a tool used by some human relations departments for screening applications for administrative positions. A cut score was not established as a requirement; each district was free to use the results in making selection decisions.

The district leaders collaborated on development of an application form that everyone would use. What they developed was a screening tool in itself, designed to ensure that those applying were serious about the effort. To provide greater insight to the planners, the application form called for significant reflection and philosophy statements. Planners were looking for individuals who had demonstrated potential for being successful leaders. Eligibility requirements included at least three years of successful teaching experience, demonstrated experience as a successful teacher leader with leadership experiences beyond the classroom level, and participation in professional development activities available in the districts to improve individual performance in the field of education. The planners looked for applicants who were truly committed to preparing themselves to be leaders.

The university partner assisted with the selection process by designing and providing distribution copies of a brochure describing the PALA and the process for applying. Districts distributed the brochures and used other methods of communication to spread the word of this opportunity for staff. Anyone meeting the published requirements was welcome to apply. The brochures announced the first class session date and included specific information about time blocks when participants would be required to attend academy sessions. Completing the application indicated a commitment to those time requirements.

It was made clear that only eight teachers would be selected in each district and that a selection committee would choose the finalists. Keeping in mind that a major purpose behind offering the academy was to increase the number of qualified applicants for leadership positions, the superintendents urged principals to identify teachers they felt were potential leaders and to encourage them to think about applying. In Jordanville, the superintendent personally suggested to several outstanding teacher leaders she worked with on other district school improvement work that they should apply. In retrospect, these personal contacts from present leaders were often the deciding factor for the teacher contemplating applying for the academy.

In all three districts, more applications were received than the academy could accommodate, and the districts were able to select those individuals they believed were most likely to become star leaders of the future. When final selections were identified but before individuals were notified, the university partner made sure all proposed members met university requirements for admission to the graduate program. A copy of the "Leadership Academy Application" (Resource G) and a sample brochure (Resource H) are included in the "Resources" section.

Identification of Partner Responsibilities

The partners reached agreement on the content and delivery of curriculum and on the general format and location of group sessions. The superintendents wanted to share responsibility for delivering instruction with university staff in the areas of their own greatest expertise, so the planning committee formed a plan for assigning responsibility for instruction among the three districts and the university faculty. The university agreed to hold academy sessions and enrollment processing at a site in one of the districts, considerably reducing the traveling distance for students. University staff members were responsible for coordinating and overseeing implementation of the instructional program.

Budgets were tight for the three districts—as usual—but the concern for quality leaders for future vacancies gave funding PALA a high priority. The superintendents believed that by collaborating, three districts would share the costs and make this an even more desirable undertaking. Still, planners had to give life to the PALA plan on a frugal budget. Funding issues were resolved for the most part at the individual district sites, but planners believed it was important for all academy participants to be treated equally, regardless of the home district. The districts agreed to share costs for all materials and supplies for students and instructors, to appoint mentors for their eight slots, and to coordinate their respective mentors. The department chair found funds for mentor stipends in his budget at the university, and academy students would be responsible for their own tuition.

In each of the two years of the academy, planners wanted participants to attend at least one out-of-district professional experience to increase understanding of the larger community. Each district agreed to cover traveling costs and to provide substitutes as needed to make participants available for designated academy activities, such as attendance at conferences and interactions between mentors and mentees. Each district decided to budget about $20,000 per year to cover their share of academy costs. However, this amount should not be considered a budget recommendation for other partnership programs. Costs would be determined by the activities included in the plan developed by the partners involved.

Each time the planners met, they constructed a written summary of the discussion in order to record the decisions made as planning proceeded. These summaries were a written accounting of the commitments made by consensus, including descriptions of how responsibilities connected to the academy would be shared among the partners. It was important for the planners to put these decisions in writing to be available as a guide to refer to during the two years of the academy. The summaries were shared with boards of education and district and university staff to keep them informed as the PALA project developed. A sample, "Planning Meeting Notes" (Resource I), is included in the "Resources" section.

The Mentoring Component

Based on the reflective comments collected from PALA participants during and at the completion of the academy, the keystone of the academy experience was the interaction between leaders-in-training and successful practitioners. (This is typical of other academy experiences.) The mentor component is where theory and practice meet. This tight connection is missing in many other models. The mentor provides guidance and support as the leader-in-training applies theory and research on best practice in authentic school settings. After considering that mentor relationships can be long-term, or a series of relationships with various positions of leadership, PALA planners chose to continue one mentor assignment throughout the academy program.

Each of the three districts determined mentor assignments as best met their needs, but the planners adopted expectations and guidelines for all mentors to follow. They put procedures in place that would regularly provide mentors with information about what was happening in the PALA group sessions. In Jordanville, the district assigned mentors who were in the same building as the leader-in-training whenever possible. There were some exceptions, such as when a principal did not meet the criteria for mentor assignments or the PALA member was not a classroom teacher assigned to a school. In the other two districts, mentors were generally not in the same buildings. While there were advantages for scheduling interactions when in the same building, most mentors located in other sites were successful in supporting their mentees. Two mentors each supported two mentees, because there were a limited number of available mentors at certain levels. Overall, the mentor connection was very positive for members of the academy. Gustafson (2005) quoted a PALA participant in a taped interview:

> My relationship with my mentor grew stronger every day, perhaps because we were in the same building. I have grown to respect the role she plays in our building so much more and I think my relationship with her will make the difference in my ability to be successful in the academy. (p. 82)

There were, however, some mentor relationships that were not as effective as others. This appeared to be the result of personality mismatches, lack of commitment on the part of mentor, or failure of the mentee to persist when scheduling time together became difficult. It was clear that performance expectations had to be developed for and shared with mentors. It was just as important that those expectations include guidelines for interacting with and supporting PALA participants throughout their work. Planners identified that more training for mentors could improve this support system.

The superintendents met with district mentors periodically and requested written input from them at benchmark points to assess the progress of members of the academy, to maintain communication, and to reinforce the importance of the mentor's role. Stipends were provided to all mentors. Copies of the "Mentoring Guidelines" (Resource J) and a sample "Request for Input From Mentors" (Resource K) are included in the "Resources" section.

The Content

The vision for the PALA academy program itself was a dynamic, fluid process that grew and evolved based on the needs, interests, and goals of the partnership and of the students involved in the program. The PALA planners were committed to keeping it that way. The committee developed an outline for the entire two-year program before the first class session convened; but like the good teacher, they knew this was a plan that would be altered and enhanced, not something set in stone.

The planners wanted to expose PALA participants to a wide range of resources, including expert practitioners and experts in theory and research. They recognized the expertise of the three superintendents involved—each had been exceptionally successful in different areas covered by the ISLLC standards being used as the foundation for this program and had served as adjunct professors for the university. One of them was recognized for leadership in improving student performance, and another had successfully passed bond issues for major facilities improvements by developing outstanding relationships with the community. The third superintendent had expertise in working with school finance. The planners made use of these resources as the curriculum was crafted and plans for delivering it took shape. They considered other personnel resources in the partner districts and members of the educational leadership faculty at the university, who, by this point, had all endorsed the new preparation program and committed to assisting with it as needed. The resulting academy program was a rich blend of school, university, and community leaders. It is worth noting that this was a distinct departure from previous leadership academy efforts, in which, according to research reported as recently as 2001, seldom were university administrative professors teaching alongside school district leaders (Gustafson, 2005).

Recognizing that one of the greatest benefits of partnering is the opportunity to influence the content of the curriculum, the planners spent much time developing the scope of study for PALA. The program they outlined was organized around the standards-based framework described previously. It included face-to-face, whole-group sessions, individual and small-group project work, attendance at conferences and other staff development events, and field experiences under the guidance of district mentors. The planners agreed there were certain activities that should be required of all academy students because these activities were important to the culture and current initiatives under way in the respective districts. They added requirements for students to observe local and state board meetings, legislative sessions, local governing bodies and other organizations related to the work of school leaders. University staff on the planning committee used these decisions to develop a syllabus for the two-year academy. In addition, there were requirements for students to be active members on school site councils or student improvement teams, demonstrating the importance of teacher leadership to leaders of continuous improvement. A list of "Required Activities" (Resource L) is included in the "Resources" section.

As the program evolved, routines emerged that added consistency to the program. For example, the agenda for whole-group sessions began to follow a common pattern. This included a regular time to discuss "hot topics" of the day. Students shared reports from the media and their own experiences and became much more aware of external influences on school operations. This was a most effective way to give leaders-in-training a broader view of the world and to prepare them for what good leaders do: anticipate the influence these events could have on local conditions. At the close of each group session, members of the class formed a circle (fishbowl) and contributed one 30-second moment of reflection on the big ideas they would take home from that evening's work. This exercise helped leaders-in-training focus on concepts as field experiences were designed. A sample "Agenda" (Resource M) is included in the "Resources" section.

As academy events unfolded, participants began expressing concern that the activities were too unstructured. They were not always sure what the instructors wanted them to do. It was some time before these leaders-in-training recognized that the lack of structured guidance was part of the planners design: to make the learning as much like the real world of leading as possible. Academy students missed the directive structure they had become accustomed to in traditional university coursework. Now, they were expected to work with mentors and academy leaders to take responsibility for their own learning experiences.

The planning committee's work continued until just before the last session of the academy at the end of the second year. They met almost monthly to review progress, add topics that might have emerged, make revisions as needed, and continue that tight connection between the training and the real work of the leaders in the schools. Planners adjusted the curriculum on the basis of individual and collective professional growth of participants, much like good teachers differentiate instruction to meet the range of students needs in the classroom. With theory and practice intertwined, PALA planners made adjustments in the original academy outline as the program evolved to focus on specific skills found to be in need of greater study or further practice. Field experiences provided invaluable information to the planners. Skills demonstrated successfully in field applications became the foundation for stretching the leader-in-training to the next-higher level of proficiency.

Assessment of Student Progress

There were frequent assessments of growth and proficiencies of performance. Authentic field experiences provided evidence of professional growth and performance skills. Reflection was the professional growth strategy emphasized, and PALA participants were required to prepare written reflections following application in practice. While instructors delivering content in class sessions determined specific measures of learning, the planning committee set standards for assessing student growth in the PALA. A portfolio, including reflections on professional growth in each of the six ISLLC standards and on the 21 McREL responsibilities, was designated as the final assessment of students' successful completion of PALA requirements. Artifacts demonstrating knowledge and performance of the standards would also be required in the portfolio.

Assessment of student progress included responses to specific assignments, reports from students and mentors on outcomes of field experiences, special presentations, and reports. Planners set benchmark assessments throughout the academy, stressing the skills identified for the program collaboratively designed by the partners. Assessments were largely performance based, with an emphasis on sharing outcomes of field experiences selected by the students and mentors to apply concept knowledge introduced in academy assignments. An emphasis was placed on student self-assessment and individual ability to take responsibility for personal professional growth. Students were also required to interact with the instructors and with each other on electronic message boards. This technology allowed them to share reflections and experiences and clarify understanding. Distance technology was also available and used in some cases to bring resource people to the academy who could not be in the same physical location.

Student conferences were an important part of the assessment process. At the midpoint of the academy, an individual student-led conference was held with each participant. The student led an interview committee in a "walk-through" of progress on the portfolio each is required to construct as documentation of the two-year program. The interview committee established performance standards in advance and measured each student interview against them. A copy of the "Leadership Academy Interview Rubric" (Resource N) is included in the "Resources" section. Students reflected verbally upon their prior year's experiences, identified strengths, and outlined professional goals for the next year.

Each student actively participated in constructing the plan for his or her own professional growth during the second academy year. Planners used the information from these conferences as they designed the next group sessions and field experiences. These interviews served as a commitment renewal for the students and provided great insight on the student's emerging leadership skills for the university and district planners to use as they collaboratively finalized the academy program for the second year. The interview team (representatives from the home district and the university) reached consensus on the status of the professional growth of the leader-in-training following the interview. A sample, "Academy Progress/End of Phase I" (Resource O), is included in the "Resources" section. Information gained regarding individual and group strengths and weaknesses at the end of the first year determined activities to be included in the second academy year.

A similar final interview was held at the end of at the end of the second year, as the final academy assessment. Gustafson (2005) interviewed

PALA participants three years after the completion of the academy and shared this quote as an example of the impact of the interview experience on the participants:

> I do not think I have ever been as nervous in my life. I knew I was prepared as I had studied my portfolio and materials from the two-year experience; however, I was afraid my mind would go blank. Fortunately, they made me feel very relaxed and part of a dynamic team when I went in there to share. (p. 88)

The completed portfolio was the individual final measure of success in the academy. The "Portfolio Evaluation Rubric for the Leadership Academy" (Resource P) is included in the "Resources" section.

Field Experiences

Throughout this book, we have emphasized how important ongoing, field-based experiences are to the theory-into-practice philosophy of the partnership academy. PALA class sessions focused on best practices in the field, research-based practices that can improve overall student performance. Given basic parameters for these field experiences (such as approval by supervisors involved), PALA students were expected to take the initiative in planning how to apply this information in activities and/or projects aligned with their own personal needs, interests, and district or building goals. We have already covered the role of mentors in the PALA program, but to emphasize their role in facilitating field experiences—mentors guided the process by making suggestions, asking questions about what might be accomplished, helping students weigh their own priorities, and guiding them through the implementation process. Because each student developed his or her own experiences, the PALA program quickly became individualized. As that occurred, the districts discovered a new source of leadership capacity they had not recognized before, and projects that might otherwise not be undertaken in the districts were accomplished as PALA students gained real-world experiences. Class sessions were used to process these experiences, reflect on the connections between theory and practice, and engage in powerful dialogue with current and prospective leaders, both students and planners.

CELEBRATIONS

PALA planners believed that leaders should celebrate successes, so each class session began with a time for participants to share celebrations. These were personal celebrations as well as celebrations of events that marked progress related to the theme of leading continuous improvement.

Celebrations included successful completion of field experiences that were of interest to the group.

At the close of the two-year program, the planners joined PALA completers and their families in a big celebration of success. University partners hosted the participants and planners at a reception honoring those who had completed the academy. PALA participants were prepared to compete for leadership positions in the future. There was also an unanticipated benefit for those leaders-in-training completing the program: They had established a support system that would be invaluable to them in the coming years, as described in this quote from a PALA graduate three years later, who was then serving in an administrative assignment:

> Whenever I am unsure, I pick up the phone and call a PALA member. I don't have to feel stupid asking my superiors and I feel confident I will get a good answer. I have 20 experts around the state who are ready to help me. If I had gone through a traditional program, I seriously doubt I would have that level of relationship with that many people, maybe one or two, but not 20. (Gustafson, 2005, p. 135)

The superintendents and the department chair celebrated the successful implementation of the plan that had begun to take form almost three years ago, when they had decided to work collaboratively on a common concern. The three districts now had an identified pool of valid candidates, standing in the wings waiting for future administrative leadership vacancies. The department chair prepared a report for the dean of his college, highlighting the successes of the PALA experiences, knowing the dean would be pleased and receptive to other applications of the partnership model. His report included these benefits, which the university gained from the partnership:

- Growing interest and enrollment in other university–public school partnership academies, which will produce a steady flow of graduate students for degrees and/or licensure in two-year cohort groups of 15 to 20 per semester
- A model for collaboration for cross-college partnerships with other departments to model collaboration
- A very natural enhancement of our professional development school model for preparing high-quality teachers for the state
- An increased ability to respond to the needs of rural districts for leadership training
- Expansion of our university outreach through the licensure of high-quality building leaders
- Expansion of our ability to provide high-quality distance education models
- A strengthened connection to the real world that enhances our preparation programs and the success of those completing them

The Jordanville superintendent was pleased as she prepared a memo to her board to summarize the PALA experience. She wanted to be sure the board members recognized the many benefits the academy had brought to the district. In the following excerpt from her memo, she told them:

> Our local district Academy participants have worked closely with mentor principals to apply their new learnings in practice. They have accepted leadership responsibilities throughout the two-year program and are now prepared to accept leadership assignments of various nature in the future, such as committee chairs, special projects, or other positions for which they might choose to apply.
>
> Each of the three districts received benefits beyond those coming from the professional growth of the students involved in the Academy. Among those benefits to our district are the following:
>
> - The district has a cadre of leaders with broader skills and commitment to call on for future school improvement efforts.
> - District leaders participating on the planning committee grew professionally as they interacted with staff and were stimulated by the responses of the PALA participants.
> - Many of the special projects completed by the participants were directly connected to school improvement efforts at the building level and produced positive results for students.
> - PALA participants shared their experiences, often with other district teachers and administrators, extending the professional growth beyond the eight directly involved in the academy.
> - Mentors cited their own growth as they worked with the PALA students in problem-solving situations.
> - University staff introduced us to additional resources that are useful in the professional growth of all of our administrative staff.
> - The close working relationship between our district and the university rose to yet another level. The direct involvement with our staff and programs has created even greater awareness of and respect for the quality present in our district.
> - There are now even more opportunities for future collaboration with the university, for the benefit of our staff and students.
> - The PALA project was featured in the recent national accreditation process for the teacher preparation program at the university, taking the positive exposure for our district even beyond our state.

Continuing to reflect on the past two years, the superintendent recalled with pleasure the frequent comments she and others had received from teachers in the academy about how this experience was making them better teachers. She thought,

> I don't want all our good teachers to abandon the classroom to pursue administrative positions, but the PALA experience was so effective in helping teachers see the bigger picture. And this made them stronger teachers in the classroom. If good teachers had experiences like this, would they become even better teachers? I think I'll call my university contact tomorrow—I wonder if a similar academy focused on teacher leadership might be possible. . . .

POSTSCRIPT ON THE PALA EXPERIENCE

The PALA story, as indicated, was told from the perspective of one of the participating districts. While some of the details in the telling of the PALA story have been altered to reflect what was learned from subsequent academy experiences, PALA did prepare 20 individuals certified to lead schools into the future. Of the 20 graduates of the academy, five years later, 9 held program coordinator or director-level positions; 10 are building principals or assistant principals (Gustafson, 2005, p. 128). The Jordanville district's positive experience with partnering led to two other academy partnerships with the university in the next five years. One of those academies targeted teacher leadership and attracted 20 individuals from classroom positions who were interested in being effective leaders while remaining in the classroom. The district continues to be recognized for outstanding accomplishments in improving student performance.

Since the PALA experience ended, all three authors are now members of the university department. We have partnered with school districts to form academies targeting preparing principals and with others targeting building teacher leadership capacity. While the PALA districts were located in close proximity to each other and to the university, we have also partnered with districts located some distance from the university and from each other. By using a variety of technological options, these partnership experiences have been equally successful.

With each academy opportunity, we have again examined our approach and reflected on how our collaborative partnership framework connects to research and best practice. Resource Q is the "Research Tracking Matrix," which shows the connections we have examined. However, our best measure of success comes from the reflections of those who participated in the academies themselves, like the quote at the beginning of this chapter and the ones below, from members of the PALA after it concluded:

> Academy has caused me to reflect deeper. My reflections now include my personal growth and what is needed for continued growth; incorporating reflective thought in my assignment, under protest, has been extremely helpful—I clearly remember the very first reflective assignment—what a chore! Now, reflective thought is

a daily part of my life, and a part I have included in the assignment of my students. The reflecting was something I will take with me into the future—asking my own students to reflect has impacted how I teach—I liked how my teachers encouraged self-direction and independent thinking. I do not look for directions from my principals as I would have 2 years ago. (Miller & Devin, 2005, pp. 2–3)

I had never given much consideration to becoming a building principal. . . . Now I think I am glad to have an opportunity to get a principal license even if I never use it. I will be a much better teacher because of this experience. (Gustafson, 2005, p. 108)

My participation in PALA was a genuine life-changing experience. I look at the entire educational field differently than I did before, because for two whole years, I got to view education from the lenses of some of the best administrators in education today. I was so fortunate. (Gustafson, 2005, p. 131)

Resources

Resource A

ISLLC Standards Summary and Sample

ISLLC Standards Summary

STANDARD I

A school leader is an educational leader who promotes the success of all students by facilitating the development, articulation, implementation, and stewardship of a **vision of learning** that is shared and supported by the school community.

STANDARD II

A school leader is an educational leader who promotes the success of all students by advocating, nurturing, and sustaining a school **culture and instructional program** conducive to student learning and staff professional growth.

STANDARD III

A school leader is an educational leader who promotes the success of all students by ensuring management of the **organization, operations, and resources** for a safe, efficient, and effective learning environment.

STANDARD IV

A school leader is an educational leader who promotes the success of all students by **collaborating** with families and community members, responding to diverse community interests and needs, and mobilizing community resources.

STANDARD V

A school leader is an educational leader who promotes the success of all students by acting with integrity and fairness and in an **ethical** manner.

STANDARD VI

A school leader is an educational leader who promotes the success of all students by understanding, responding to, and influencing the **larger political, social, economic, legal, and cultural context**.

The full standards are defined by a combination of knowledge, disposition, and performance indicators.

Copies of the complete standards can be ordered from:

Council of Chief State School Officers
Attn: Publications
One Massachusetts Avenue, NW, Suite 700
Washington, DC 200001-1431
Phone: (202) 336-7016

You can view the complete standards on the Internet at http://www.ccsso.org/content/pdfs/isllcstd.pdf.

ISLLC Standards Sample

STANDARD I

A school administrator is an educational leader who promotes the success of all students by facilitating the development, articulation, implementation, and stewardship of a vision of learning that is shared and supported by the school community.

Knowledge

The administrator has knowledge and understanding of the

- Learning goals in a pluralistic society
- The principles of developing and implementing strategic plans
- Systems theory
- Information sources, data collection, and data analysis strategies
- Effective communication
- Effective consensus building and negotiation skills

Dispositions

The administrator believes in, values, and is committed to

- The educability of all
- A school vision of high standards of learning
- Continuous school improvement
- The inclusion of all members of the school community
- Ensuring that students have the knowledge, skills, and values needed to become successful adults
- A willingness to continuously examine one's own assumptions, beliefs, and practices
- Doing the work required for high levels of personal and organization performance

Performances

The administrator facilitates processes and engages in activities to ensuring that

- The vision and mission of the school are effectively communicated to staff, parents, students, and community members.

- The vision and mission are communicated through the use of symbols, ceremonies, stories, and similar activities.
- The core beliefs of the school vision are modeled for all stakeholders.
- The vision is developed with and among stakeholders.
- The contributions of school community members to the realization of the vision are recognized and celebrated.
- Progress toward the vision and mission is communicated to all stakeholders.
- The school community is involved in school improvement efforts.
- The vision shapes the educational programs, plans, and activities.
- The vision shapes the educational programs, plans, and actions.
- An implementation plan is developed in which objectives and strategies to achieve the vision and goals are clearly articulated
- Assessment data related to student learning are used to develop the school vision and goals.
- Relevant demographic data pertaining to students and their families are used in developing the school mission and goals.
- Barriers to achieving the vision are identified, clarified, and addressed.
- Needed resources are sought and obtained to support the implementation of the school mission and goals.
- Existing resources are used in support of the school vision and goals.
- The vision, mission, and implementation plans are regularly monitored, evaluated, and revised.

SOURCE: Council of Chief State School Officers. (1996). *Interstate School Leaders Licensure Consortium (ISLLC) Standards for School Leaders*. Washington, DC: Author. Available: http://www.ccsso.org/content/pdfs/isllcstd.pdf.

The Interstate School Leaders Licensure Consortium (ISLLC) Standards for School Leaders (Council of Chief State School Officers, 1996) were written by representatives from states and professional associations in a partnership with the National Policy Board for Educational Administration in 1994–95, supported by grants from the Pew Charitable Trusts and the Danforth Foundation. The standards were published by the Council of Chief State School Officers, copyright © 1996 and are currently being updated.

Resource B

McREL's 21 Responsibilities of School Leaders

Balanced Leadership Framework Responsibilities, Average *r*, and Associated Practices

Responsibilities	*Average* r	*Practices Associated With Responsibilities*
Affirmation	.19	• Systematically and fairly recognizes and celebrates accomplishments of teachers and staff • Systematically and fairly recognizes and celebrates accomplishments of students • Systematically and fairly acknowledges failures and celebrates accomplishments of the school
Change Agent	.25	• Consciously challenges the status quo • Is comfortable leading change initiatives with uncertain outcomes • Systematically considers new and better ways of doing things
Communication	.23	• Is easily accessible to teachers and staff
	.24	• Develops effective means for teachers and staff to communicate with one another
		• Maintains open and effective lines of communication with teachers and staff

Responsibilities	*Average* r	*Practices Associated With Responsibilities*
Contingent Rewards	.24	• Recognizes individuals who excel • Uses performance vs. seniority as the primary criterion for reward and advancement • Uses hard work and results as the basis for reward and recognition
Culture	.25	• Promotes cooperation among teachers and staff • Promotes a sense of well-being • Promotes cohesion among teachers and staff • Develops an understanding of purpose • Develops a shared vision of what the school could be like
Curriculum, Instruction, Assessment	.20	• Is involved with teachers in designing curricular activities and addressing instructional issues in their classrooms. • Is involved with teachers to address assessment issues
Discipline	.27	• Protects instructional time from interruptions • Protects/shelters teachers from distractions
Flexibility	.28	• Is comfortable with major changes in how things are done • Encourages people to express opinions that may be contrary to those held by individuals in positions of authority • Adapts leadership style to needs of specific situations • Can be directive or nondirective as the situation warrants
Focus	.24	• Establishes high, concrete goals and the expectation that all students will meet them • Establishes high, concrete goals for all curricula, instruction, and assessment • Establishes high, concrete goals for the general functioning of the school • Keeps everyone's attention focused on established goals
Ideals/Beliefs	.22	• Holds strong professional ideals and beliefs about schooling, teaching, and learning • Shares ideals and beliefs about schooling, teaching, and learning with teachers, staff, and parents • Demonstrates behaviors that are consistent with ideals and beliefs

(Continued)

(Continued)

Responsibilities	*Average* r	*Practices Associated With Responsibilities*
Input	.25	• Provides opportunities for input from teachers and staff on all important decisions • Provides opportunities for teachers and staff to be involved in policy development • Involves the school leadership team in decision making
Intellectual Stimulation	.24	• Stays informed about current research and theory regarding effective schooling • Continually exposes teachers and staff to cutting-edge ideas about how to be effective • Systematically engages teachers and staff in discussions about current research and theory • Continually involves teachers and staff in reading articles and books about effective practices
Knowledge of Curriculum, Instruction, Assessment	.25	• Is knowledgeable about curriculum and instructional practices • Is knowledgeable about assessment practices • Provides conceptual guidance for teachers regarding effective classroom practice
Monitors/ Evaluates	.27	• Monitors and evaluates the effectiveness of the curriculum • Monitors and evaluates the effectiveness of instruction • Monitors and evaluates the effectiveness of assessment
Optimizer	.20	• Inspires teachers and staff to accomplish things that might seem beyond their grasp • Portrays a positive attitude about the ability of teachers and staff to accomplish substantial things • Is a driving force behind major initiatives
Order	.25	• Provides and enforces clear structures, rules, and procedures for teachers, staff, and students • Establishes routines regarding the running of the school that teachers and staff understand and follow • Ensures that the school is in compliance with district and state mandates
Outreach	.27	• Advocates on behalf of the school in the community • Interacts with parents in ways that enhance their support for the school • Ensures that the central office is aware of the school's accomplishments

Responsibilities	*Average* r	*Practices Associated With Responsibilities*
Relationships	.18	• Remains aware of personal needs of teachers and staff • Maintains personal relationships with teachers and staff • Is informed about significant personal issues in the lives of teachers and staff • Acknowledges significant events in the lives of teachers and staff
Resources	.25	• Ensures that teachers and staff have necessary materials and equipment • Ensures that teachers have necessary professional development opportunities that directly enhance their teaching
Situational Awareness	.33	• Is aware of informal groups and relationships among teachers and staff • Is aware of issues in the school that have not surfaced, but could create discord • Can predict what could go wrong from day to day
Visibility	.20	• Makes systematic and frequent visits to classrooms • Is highly visible around the school • Has frequent contact with students

SOURCE: Waters, T., & Grubb, S. (2004). *Leading Schools: Distinguishing the Essential From the Important*. Colorado: McREL.

NOTE: The *r* correlations reported in this table were derived from McREL's leadership meta-analysis.

Resource C

Matrix Combining ISLLC Standards and McREL's 21 Responsibilities

McREL's 21 Responsiblities[1]	*ISLLC Standards*[2]					
	I	*II*	*III*	*IV*	*V*	*VI*
Affirmation		X			X	
Change Agent	X	X		X		
Communication	X		X	X		X
Contingent Rewards		X			X	
Culture	X	X	X		X	
Curriculum, Instruction, Assessment		X		X		
Discipline		X	X	X		
Flexibility			X	X		X
Focus		X		X		X
Ideas, Beliefs	X	X			X	X
Input			X	X		X
Intellectual Stimulation	X					X
Knowledge of Curriculum, Instruction, Assessment	X		X		X	
Monitors, Evaluates	X	X				X
Optimizer	X			X		X
Order		X	X			
Outreach				X	X	X
Relationship	X	X	X	X	X	X
Resources			X	X		X
Situational Awareness			X		X	X
Visibility			X	X		X

SOURCES

1. Waters, T., & Grubb, S. (2004). *Leading Schools: Distinguishing the Essential From the Important.* Colorado: McREL.
2. Council of Chief State School Officers. (1996). *Interstate School Leaders Licensure Consortium (ISLLC) Standards for School Leaders.* Washington, DC: Author. Available: http://www.ccsso .org/content/pdfs/isllcstd.pdf.

The Interstate School Leaders Licensure Consortium (ISLLC) Standards for School Leaders (Council of Chief State School Officers, 1996) were written by representatives from states and professional associations in a partnership with the National Policy Board for Educational Administration in 1994–95, supported by grants from the Pew Charitable Trusts and the Danforth Foundation. The standards were published by the Council of Chief State School Officers, copyright © 1996 and are currently being updated.

Resource D

Matrix Combining ISLLC Standards and NPBEA 21 Competencies

	ISLLC Standards[2]					
Competency[1]	*I*	*II*	*III*	*IV*	*V*	*VI*
Leadership	X	X	X	X	X	X
Information Collection			X			X
Problem Analysis			X			X
Judgment	X	X		X	X	X
Organizational Oversight			X			
Implementation		X	X			
Delegation	X		X	X		
Instruction and Learning Environment		X				
Curriculum Design		X				
Student Guidance and Development		X			X	
Staff Development		X	X			
Measurement and Evaluation			X			
Resource Allocation		X	X			
Motivating Others	X				X	
Interpersonal Sensitivity	X				X	
Oral and Nonverbal Expression				X		X
Written Expression	X	X				
Philosophical and Cultural Values					X	
Legal and Regulatory Applications			X			X
Policy and Political Influences						X
Public Relations	X			X		

SOURCES

1. National Policy Board for Educational Administration. (1993). *Principles for Our Changing Schools: Knowledge and Skills Base.* Fairfax, Virginia: NPBEA.

2. Council of Chief State School Officers. (1996). *Interstate School Leaders Licensure Consortium (ISLLC) Standards for School Leaders.* Washington, DC: Author. Available: http://www .ccsso.org/content/ pdfs/isllcstd.pdf.

   The Interstate School Leaders Licensure Consortium (ISLLC) Standards for School Leaders (Council of Chief State School Officers, 1996) were written by representatives from states and professional associations in a partnership with the National Policy Board for Educational Administration in 1994–95, supported by grants from the Pew Charitable Trusts and the Danforth Foundation. The standards were published by the Council of Chief State School Officers, copyright © 1996 and are currently being updated.

Resource E

Importance/Urgency Organizer

STANDARD II

A school administrator is an educational leader who promotes the success of all students by advocating, nurturing, and sustaining a school culture and instructional program conducive to student learning and staff professional growth.

	High Importance	*Moderate Importance*
High Urgency *Low Urgency*	• All individuals are treated with fairness, dignity, and respect. • Professional development promotes a focus on student learning consistent with the school vision and goals. • Students and staff feel valued and important. • Barriers to student learning are identified, clarified, and addressed. • There is a culture of high expectations for self, student, and staff performance. • The school is organized and aligned for success. • Curriculum and decisions are based on research, expertise of teachers, and the recommendations of learned societies. • Student learning is assessed using a variety of techniques. • Lifelong learning is encouraged and modeled. • The school culture and climate are assessed on a regular basis. • A variety of sources of information are used to make decisions. • A variety of supervisory and evaluation models are employed. • Pupil personnel programs are developed to meet the needs of students and their families. • Diversity is considered in developing learning experiences.	• The responsibilities and contributions of each individual are acknowledged. • Technologies are used in teaching and learning. • Student and staff accomplishments are recognized and celebrated. • Multiple opportunities to learn are available to all students. • Curricular, cocurricular, and extracurricular programs are designed, implemented, evaluated, and refined. • Multiple sources of information regarding performance are used by staff and students.

Resource F

Planning Framework by ISLLC Standard

ISLLC STANDARD I: VISION OF LEARNING

A school administrator is an educational leader who promotes the success of all students by facilitating the development, articulation, implementation, and the stewardship of a vision of learning that is shared and supported by the school community.

Time Allotment: 15%

Competency Areas

Leadership, Judgment, Delegation, Motivating Others, Written Expression, Public Relations, Interpersonal Sensitivity

ISLLC/ETS Frameworks for School Leaders

Standard I: The Vision of Learning

- Developing the Vision
- Communicating the Vision
- Implementing the Vision
- Monitoring and Evaluating the Vision

From Balanced Leadership 21 Responsibilities

Culture, Communication, Relationship, Change Agent, Optimizer, Ideals/Beliefs, Monitors/Evaluates, Intellectual Stimulation

Context: School/District

Topics

Systems Theory

Strategic Planning

Learning Goals

Communication Skills

Consensus Building

Negotiations

Required Activities

- Attend at least one local board of education meeting each year.
- Attend a site council meeting and a faculty meeting in another building at least once each year.
- Participate on the site council in your building for at least one year.
- Attend at least one bargaining session each year.

Materials/Resources

Asking the Right Questions Toolkit, McREL (http://www.mcrel.org/toolkit/)

Leadership Sustainability, Michael Fullan (2005)

School Leadership That Works: From Research to Results, Robert Marzano, Timothy Waters, & Brian McNulty (2005)

Resource G

Leadership Academy Application

QUALIFICATIONS

Candidates will be expected to meet the university admission requirements. Successful candidates for admission to the academy will be able to demonstrate the following:

1. At least one year of successful teaching. Preference will be given to teachers with three or more years of successful teaching experiences
2. Understanding of the process of school improvement and a commitment to lifelong learning
3. Knowledge of good instruction and willingness to apply the research on best practice
4. Potential as a successful leader
5. Participation in professional development activities designed to improve individual performance in the field of education
6. Commitment to leadership at multiple levels and to service within the district
7. Commitment to participate in the requirements of this program

SECTION I. PERSONAL DATA

Name ______________________________________ SS# ______________
Last First M.I.

Address ____
Street City State Zip

Telephone Number (Home) ________________ (Work) ________________

SECTION II. EXPERIENCE AND EMPLOYMENT HISTORY

Beginning with most recent, list full-time/part-time or summer school experience in an accredited K–12 public or private school. List any unique job responsibilities that demonstrate leadership potential.

Position:	From: To:	List relevant job responsibilities:
School:		1. 2.
Address:		3. 4.
Supervisor:		5. 6.
Telephone:		7.

Position:	From: To:	List relevant job responsibilities:
School:		1. 2.
Address:		3. 4.
Supervisor:		5. 6.
Telephone:		7.

Position:	From: To:	List relevant job responsibilities:
School:		1. 2.
Address:		3. 4.
Supervisor:		5. 6.
Telephone:		7.

Position:	From: To:	List relevant job responsibilities:
School:		1. 2.
Address:		3. 4.
Supervisor:		5. 6.
Telephone:		7.

Please explain any gaps in employment:

____

____

____

SECTION III. EDUCATION

Transcriptions should be submitted if not already on file with the district.

A. Degrees

Degrees Received	*University*	*Date*

B. Courses Earned After Completion of Last Degree

Course	*Hours*	*University*	*Date*

SECTION IV. ELIGIBILITY

Respond to the following statements. Please be thorough but brief and limit your responses to no more than three attached pages for Section IV.

1. Provide evidence of your effectiveness at your current assignment, including your knowledge of instruction and some evidence of the effectiveness of your instruction.
2. Describe how you use research on best practices to help you improve your effectiveness in making sure students are successful.
3. Describe experiences you have had as a leader at the building level.
4. List the professional development strands you have participated in and/or implemented during the past three years.
5. Describe an experience that demonstrates your ability to work effectively with others.
6. Describe any leadership opportunities you have had beyond the building level. You can include district and/or community activities.
7. Write a one-paragraph response to each of the following:
   a. My personal philosophy of education is . . .
   b. I am interested in improving my leadership skills because . . .
   c. My professional goal is . . .
8. List reasons you should be selected for this academy.
9. If selected, describe the commitment you would bring to the program.

SECTION V. ATTACHMENTS TO THE APPLICATION

1. On a separate page, compose a memorandum to staff members informing them of a meeting to revise the present plan for improving student achievement. Tell them attendance at this meeting is mandatory.
2. Provide two letters of recommendation. At least one should be from a public school administrator who has supervised your work.

Resource H

Brochure

Sample

Funding

Candidates will pay for their own college tuition and will need to commit some evenings, weekends, and time during two summers to the process. The Professional Administrative Leadership Academy will consist of 39 graduate credits. Tuition will be paid in six or seven installments during the two-year program. The school districts will provide some release time for professional development, textbooks, material, supplies, and internship opportunities for participants.

Our State University

Notice of Non-discrimination

Morrisburg Public Schools

Questions may be directed to:

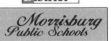

Superintendent
USD #
Jordanville Schools
Phone #

Superintendent
USD #
Silverton Schools
Phone #

Superintendent
USD #
Morrisburg Schools
Phone #

Chair
Educational Administration and Leadership
Phone #
name@email.edu

Liaison
Phone #
name@email.edu

Leadership Academy

Principals Administrative Leadership Academy (PALA)

and

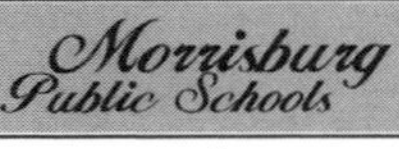

and

and

The Department of Educational Leadership

Academy
Principals Administrative Leadership Academy (PALA)

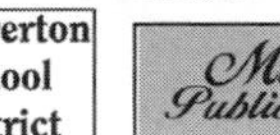

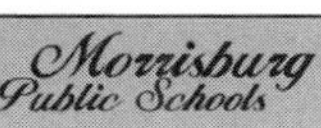

Program

Three school districts (Jordanville, Silverton, and Morrisburg) will partner with Our State University to deliver a high caliber "field-based" administrative training academy. Students who successfully complete the two-year program will earn a master's degree from OSU. This academy is expected to develop quality candidates for administrative positions to address shortages and provide stability to three districts (Jordanville, Silverton, and Morrisburg) and assure that a pool of candidates will be available in the future as veteran leaders retire.

Program Themes

Participants will be involved in several significant district assigned learning sequences/projects that will be of benefit to both the district and the participant. The projects may include, but are not limited to, curriculum design, program evaluation, research studies, school improvement strategies, personnel, school finance and business, technology integration, and strategic planning processes. In addition, participants will be asked to research and explore exemplary practices and possible solutions for major social issues facing school districts and communities.

Curriculum Alignment

Proficiency in standards set forth by the Interstate School Leaders Licensure Consortium (ISLLC), The Curriculum Guidelines for Advanced Programs in Educational Leadership from the National Council for Accreditation of Teacher Education (NCATE) and the 21 competency areas formulated by the National Policy Board for Educational Administration.

Candidates will also communicate and do research work utilizing the Internet. Some coursework and assignments may be available on an academy Web site.

Mentors

Each successful candidate will work with skilled mentors within or outside their school district. Mentors will be selected on the basis of their expertise related to program themes and potential projects. The purpose of the mentors is to assist candidates in analyzing ideas and working on special projects identified in the Leadership Academy.

Faculty

Instructional delivery will be shared between the faculty of the Educational Administration and Leadership department at OSU and administrators and guest lecturers furnished by the three districts. In addition, a large part of the instruction will be delivered by veteran school administrators currently employed by the districts.

Program Description

The program will include two phases:

- **Phase I** will begin in early March and end in late February.
- **Phase II** will begin in early March and end in late February. All participants will need to re-apply for Phase II. Continuance in the program will be based upon assessment and individualized growth plans.

Application for Admission

Application Criteria

All applicants will be evaluated on their readiness for the academy and potential for sustained leadership success in USD #/#/# and beyond. Applicants must be able to meet the admission requirements for the Graduate School at Our State University.

The successful candidate for admission to the PALA will be able to demonstrate the following:

1. At least one year of successful teaching. Preference will be given to teachers with three or more years of successful teaching experience.
2. Understanding of the process of school improvement and a commitment to lifelong learning.
3. Demonstrated knowledge of good instruction and willingness to apply the research on best practice.
4. Demonstrated potential as a successful teacher leader.
5. Participation in professional development activities designed to improve individual performance in the field of education.
6. Commitment to leadership at multiple levels, and to service in USD #/#/#.
7. A commitment to participate in the requirements in selected phases of the program.

Application Process

Each district will select 8 (24 total) aspiring professionals for the Academy. The candidates must have a minimum of three years of successful teaching experience and be able to meet the admission requirements for the Graduate School at Our State University.

Applications are due by February 1, at 5:00 PM. to the personnel office in each district.

Resource I

Planning Meeting Notes

Sample

June 1, 2007

To: District Superintendent

From: University Partner

Subject: New Academy

Thanks for visiting with us yesterday about the concept of a leadership academy for your district. As the department chair shared with you earlier, our State University College of Education is delighted that you are interested in partnering on this academy experience. The purpose of this memorandum is to summarize our conversation in your office on June 1, as we began the planning process for Academy X.

I have attempted to record the highlights of our discussion in the statements below. Please let me know if you would suggest any changes, so that we can all be comfortable with this as an accurate record for future reference. You will note, however, that I have added some comments as I thought about our first planning meeting on July 6, so that you and your staff might be thinking about issues we will need to address. Feel free to let me know of changes you would prefer or other items you would like to see added. Our goal is to develop an academy structure that meets university and state requirements, but within a context that directly supports goals for your district.

PURPOSE/GENERAL DESCRIPTION OF A NEW ACADEMY

- The purpose of the new academy would be to provide an opportunity for staff to complete requirements for a master's degree in administration and an entry to the state licensure at the building level.
- This will be a two-year cohort group; participants will reapply for continuing participation in Year 2.
- The first meeting of the academy will be in a January/February time frame. An ending date for the academy will be determined as details are planned in the coming months.
- The academy will accommodate approximately 20 participants. We will target those beginning or in the early stages of the master's program in educational leadership.
- Other applicants will be considered on a case-by-case basis.

RESPONSIBILITIES OF THE PARTNERS

- The partner responsibilities for the new academy will be similar to previous arrangements. Specifics will be identified during the planning process.

District

- Continue to provide the following as for past academies: books/materials, meeting space, refreshments/light meals, copying/printing services, supplies, limited secretarial support.
- Provide some release time (as established during the planning process) for academy participants.
- Assign mentors as determined by the planning committee.
- Send academy participants to Council for Public School Improvement (CPSI) sessions as part of the class schedule.
- Select district administrators to participate in planning the academy program.
- Provide staff with appropriate expertise to assist in the delivery of and support needed to implement the program established by the planning committee.

University Staff

- Coordinate the program and facilitate enrollment procedures.
- Manage degree and licensure requirements.
- Contribute the latest research information on preparation for building leadership.
- Assume responsibility for class sessions.

PLANNING FOR THE NEW ACADEMY

- Planning will begin immediately and continue through the first semester of the 2007–2008 school year. It is expected the planning committee will meet as often as needed to confirm plans for the two-year program before the first session of the academy. Once class sessions begin, the planning committee will meet once each month (or as needed) for the duration of the academy program.
- The following timeline is suggested for discussion purposes:

July 6	First Planning Meeting
August/September	Announcement of coming academy
NLT October 23	Applications out to staff
November 15	Applications close
NLT December	Participants selected
January/February	First class session

NLT: No later than

SUGGESTED AGENDA ITEMS FOR FIRST PLANNING MEETING, JULY 6

Location: Superintendent's Office, 8:30 a.m.

- University staff attending
- District superintendent and staff as selected by the superintendent

Possible Agenda Items for Discussion

- Establish meeting dates for Planning Committee work.
- Identify focus and themes for the academy curriculum of study.
- Establish priorities for selecting participants.
- Consider who will be actively involved in planning, in academy activities, and in support systems.
- Discuss how to connect the academy program to other professional development priorities and themes in the district.
- Discuss possible frameworks for mentoring support.
- Consider materials for Year 1 and Year 2.
- Other items.

Resource J

Mentoring Guidelines

PROFESSIONAL EDUCATIONAL LEADERSHIP ACADEMY

Statement of Purpose of the Mentor Assignments

The purpose of the relationship between the mentor and the mentee is to support the academy's effort to provide multifaceted experiences that strengthen the participant's preparation toward a career in educational administration.

Expectations of Mentors

The role of the mentor is to facilitate the mentee's authentic experiences in applying the leadership skills studied in academy sessions:

- Have a basic knowledge of the ISLLC standards.
- Meet regularly with mentee to answer questions, discuss topics, and advise.
- Assist the mentee in successfully planning and completing projects to experience leadership situations.
- Observe growth in professional leadership qualities or concerns thereof and share your observations with academy leaders, as requested, to assist in planning and assessing the participant's progress in the preparation program.
- Conference with the mentee as he or she develops goals and projects for each standard.
- Periodically read the mentee's reflection about projects.

Expectation of Mentees

The role of the mentee is to keep the mentor informed of topics discussed in academy sessions and to initiate conversations about projects that are designed to build performance skills in each standard area:

- Take the initiative to make contacts and schedule time with your mentor.
- Share academy materials with mentors.
- Explain the standards as they are studied and share your ideas about goals and projects that relate to that standard.
- Practice leadership roles in your mentor's building (and/or your building, if different than mentor's).
- Keep a journal of meetings with your mentor and reflect on your growth.

Expectations of Local District Leaders

The role of local district leaders is to assist mentors and mentees, as needed, to make the projects the most meaningful in preparation for academy students and the most beneficial to the school district operations:

- Touch base periodically with mentors to discuss the mentee's progress and projects.
- Assist mentors in their efforts to work effectively with mentees.
- Provide guidelines, as necessary, for mentors to use in facilitating project work designed by the mentee for each standard.

Expectations of University Academy Leaders

The role of the university academy leaders is to assist mentors, mentees, and local district leaders in making the Professional Educational Leadership Academy as meaningful a preparation as possible for the participants and the district.

- Meet with mentors to explain the expectations of the relationship.
- Prepare mentees for the mentor relationship.
- Provide materials as necessary to assist the mentor-mentee relationships.
- Request feedback from the mentors that will be helpful in developing the best preparation program possible for each academy participant.

Resource K

Request for Input From Mentors

Sample

PROFESSIONAL ADMINISTRATIVE LEADERSHIP ACADEMY

End of Year 1 Assessment

Guiding Questions for Mentors

Mentors should complete one copy of these questions for each participant mentored during the first year.

PALA Participant Mentored ______________________________

Mentor ____

Date ___________

1. How has this participant shown the initiative, commitment, and quality performance required for a career in educational administration during your work together the past year? (If you have not observed these qualities, please note that as your response.)

2. How has this individual demonstrated understanding of what is involved and the potential for being a successful building-level school administrator in your work together?

3. What areas have you seen to be strengths in this individual?

4. What areas do you recommend be emphasized for growth in the second year of this program?

5. Do you believe this participant will be a strong candidate for leadership positions in our district in the future? Please comment on any reservations you have about this person's ability to be successful in such a position.

6. Do you recommend this person be invited to continue in Year 2 of the Professional Administrative Leadership Academy?

   Yes, without reservation _______ No _______

   Yes, but with the following reservation(s):

7. If you wish to do so, add comments here.

Resource L

Required Activities

Each of the activities below is **required of all academy participants.** You should complete at least four of these during the first year. Note some state that the activity must be repeated each year. Write a reflection for each experience from the perspective of a neutral observer. See directions for preparing reflections below:

- Attend one meeting of the Board of Education **each year.**
- Attend one site council meeting in a building other than the one you work in.
- Attend one faculty meeting in a building other than the one you work in.
- Attend at least one bargaining session **each year.**
- Attend a meeting of the City Commission.
- Attend one meeting of the State Board of Education.
- Attend at least one session of the mentor training during the first Academy Year.
- Attend a meeting of the Curriculum and Instruction Advisory Council as an observer and reflect on the process as a strategy for school improvement.

GUIDELINES FOR PREPARING REFLECTIONS FROM THE PERSPECTIVE OF A NEUTRAL OBSERVER

Reflections should include your name and clearly identify the activity and the date it occurred, and should be written from your perspective as an observer of the event. An observer is not an active participant in the meeting.

A reflection is not the same as the minutes of the meeting and does not offer judgment on individual participants.

The reflection should focus on the process and behavior of those participating. Observations might include making connections to elements in our study, commenting on the leadership models, group dynamics, and indications of effective teamwork.

Questions that may be addressed include the following: What was the purpose of the meeting? Did members seem to be aware of that purpose or to be committed to a common goal? Was the purpose accomplished? What leadership approach was used? How did participants react to it? How does this activity contribute to the organization's goals?

One copy of the reflection should be turned in when it is completed.

Another copy should be included in a special section of your portfolio.

Reflections are due no later than the last class session in Fall 2007 for Year 1 and the last class session in Fall 2008 for Year 2.

This list may be revised.

ADDITIONAL ACTIVITIES: CHOOSE ANY FOUR

Each academy participant is required to participate in **at least four additional activities** sometime within the two years of the academy. For each completed activity, prepare a written reflection on your professional growth from the experience, focusing on what you learned from the experience that will help you as a leader of school improvement. For instructions on these professional growth reflections, see below:

- Serve on a site council. (You may serve in your building as a staff member or in another as a parent or community representative.)
- Participate in a leadership role on a district-level curriculum task force or text selection committee sometime during the course of the academy. You may do this during the school year or during summer curriculum work.
- Working with your principal, participate in the planning and delivery of at least one staff development day during the course of the academy. Evaluate and reflect on that day, formulating suggestions for improvement.
- At some time during the two-year academy, help form and participate in a book study group, using a book you assist the group in selecting because of its value to the group's efforts to eliminate the achievement gap in student performance.

- Attend the state's budget workshop in June.
- Working with the human resources office, attend a recruitment fair sometime during the two-year academy.
- Select a special activity with prior approval of an academy instructor.

GUIDELINES FOR PREPARING REFLECTIONS FOCUSING ON PROFESSIONAL GROWTH

Reflections should identify the activity and the date it occurred. They are not a log or listing of activities. (You may wish to keep such a log or listing for other purposes, but do not include those in the reflection.) You will be reflecting on the effectiveness of your own participation and on the success of the group in accomplishing the task assigned.

Appropriate questions might include the following: Did all members participate? Did the group accomplish its mission? How will others receive the group's work product? What impact will the group's decision have on the system? What seemed to work best for the group? What might have changed to make the experience more effective? What did you personally learn from the experience? How will this affect what you do in the future?

One copy of the reflection should be turned in when it is completed.

Another copy should be included in a special section of your portfolio.

Reflections are due no later than the last class session in Fall 2007 for Year 1 and the last class session in Fall 2008 for Year 2.

This list may be revised.

Resource M

Agenda

Sample

PROFESSIONAL EDUCATIONAL LEADERSHIP ACADEMY

March 9

Assignments Due:

Writing Assignment Due March 9

Address the following:

The Kind of Building Leader I Want to Be

Reflect on the various examples and discussions of leadership in our work so far. How have they influenced your vision of building leadership? Is your vision of the building leader aligned with your personal philosophy of education?

Systems-Thinking Assignment From McREL Web Site

Turn In to Instructor

- Written reflection on this planning-tool Web site
- Have copies to share

Reform Initiative

- Implementing an initiative using guiding questions
- Resource sites for systems planners

Agenda

1. Opening Comments
2. Whip Activities
3. Celebrations
4. Questions/Comments on Academy Work
   a. Brain-Based Research Seminar Presentation
   b. Online
5. Hot Topics
6. Guest Expert: Architect

   A review of building projects under way: How leaders interact with architects in planning and implementing projects
7. Discussion of Systems Thinking: *Asking the Right Questions Toolkit* work (http://www.mcrel.org/toolkit/)
8. Standards 1–3: *Leading Learning Communities* (NAESP, 2001)

Online Assignments

Check out at least two Web sites from the end of sections on Standards 1–3 and be prepared to share them in class March 9. Describe what the site contains and how it might be helpful to leaders of learning communities.

9. An introduction to interest-based bargaining: A problem-solving approach to managing conflict
10. Reflection (Fishbowl): What big ideas do we take away from tonight's session?

Assignments

- Volunteers for next week's whip activity
- Watch for developments related to school finance
- Read Standards 4 and 5 in *Leading Learning Communities*

Questions About Future Class Dates

April 27: State Department of Education Conference, Change Game.

Resource N

Leadership Academy Interview Rubric

The "end of Phase I" (and II) interview will be completed collaboratively with you and representatives from the university and public school planners in attendance. Please allow an hour for the interview and use the time to share your reflections, identify key learning experiences, discuss your growth and self-assessment in relationship to the standards, and answer questions from the planners. Ratings will be made collaboratively by the planners to determine the overall ratings and then will be shared with you in written form following the interview.

	Awareness	*Emerging*	*Proficient*	*Distinguished*
Evidence of growth in knowledge of teacher leadership				
Evidence of growth in performance as a teacher leader				
Demonstration of understanding of the standards				
Evidence of performance of the standards				
Ability to project needs for future growth and articulate ways to address those needs				
Meets portfolio requirements				

General Comments:

Overall Rating:

Resource O

Academy Progress/ End of Phase I

Sample

Evidence of Growth in Knowledge of Teacher Leadership	*Level of Performance*			
	Awareness	*Emerging*	*Proficient*	*Distinguished*
Student A		X——	——X	
Student B			X	
Student C		X——	——X	
Student D		X——	——X	
Student E		X		
Student F		X——	——X	
Student G				X
Student H		X		
Student I		X——	——X	
Student J			—X	
Student K		X——X		
Student L	X——	——	——X	
Student M		X——	——X	
Student N				X
Student O		X——	——X	
Student P		X——	——X	
Student Q	X——	——X		
Student R		X——	——	——X

NOTE: Progress bars show the range of student progress from "Awareness" to "Distinguished" during the term of Phase I.

Resource P

Portfolio Evaluation Rubric for the Leadership Academy

Student's Name ____________________ Evaluator ____________________

Semester Fall 07 08 09 10 Summer 07 08 09 10

Spring 07 08 09 10

OVERALL PERFORMANCE

The evaluator should rate each of the items as listed below:

3	*2*	*1*	*0*
Excellent, exceeds expectations	Satisfactory, meets expectations	Needs revision	Fails to meet minimal expectations and needs more than just moderate to minor revisions

Rating	*Criteria*
______	Used APA style to cite professional literature (*Publication Manual of the American Psychological Association,* 2001, 5th ed.).
______	Integrated knowledge from all educational leadership content areas.
______	Emphasized the application of theory and research to practice.
______	Did not use collaborators or editors.
______	Followed university policy regarding plagiarism and academic dishonesty.
______	Included all required sections (résumé, program of studies, artifact descriptions, showcased artifacts, pre/mid/post self-assessments, synthesized reflection statement, detailed reflections on each of the six standards).
______	Artifact descriptions contained sufficient details to determine student's role and nature of the artifact.
______	Showcased artifacts had strong, appropriate rationale for inclusion.
______	Self-assessments indicated good self-awareness.
______	All six standards reflections provided sufficient details to determine levels of attainment.
______	The synthesized growth statement accurately interpreted and documented growth.

RUBRIC FOR SELF-ASSESSMENT MATRIX/STANDARDS I–VI

Perceptions of Growth and Final Level of Attainment by Knowledge, Dispositions, and Performances for Each ISLLC Standard

One member of the assessment team will record the student's perceived growth for Standard I by giving a numerical rating that reflects the change in the student's ranking and the letter of the highest rating. For example, a student who perceives growth across two categories, from "Little Understanding" to "Proficient," would be marked "2P"; a student who perceives growth across one category, from "Basic" to "Proficient," would be marked with a "1P"; a student who perceives no growth would be noted with the letter of rating and no number (to indicate no growth perceived in that category). LU = Little Understanding; B = Basic Understanding; P = Proficient; D = Distinguished.

Sample Rating

Student	*Category*	*Std. I*	*Std. II*	*Std. III*	*Std. IV*	*Std. V*	*Std. VI*
A	Knowledge	B	B	1P	B	B	B
	Dispositions	1P	1P	B	B	2P	B
	Performances	B	P	B	1P	B	2D

Student	*Category*	*Std. I*	*Std. II*	*Std. III*	*Std. IV*	*Std. V*	*Std. VI*
A	Knowledge						
	Dispositions						
	Performances						

RUBRIC FOR SHOWCASED ARTIFACTS/STANDARDS I–VI

Strong	*Acceptable*	*Marginal/Needs Revision*
Student has included multiple, well-articulated details describing his or her role in the leadership activity and how the selected artifact fits the standard. The artifact reflects a clear leadership role, a strong contribution by the student, and collaboration with others.	Student has included sufficient details with adequate articulation. The selected artifact fits the standard, but does not reflect a dominant leadership role by the student. Student was involved in a minor role or given a project with directions for completion.	Student attended activities, but the leadership role is not clear, with no evidence of the contribution. Artifact reflects minimal initiative, clerical duties, or nothing distinctly different from his or her current teaching position. Student does not give a rationale for use of this artifact as evidence for the standard.

Standard	*Rating*	*Comments*
Standard I		
Standard II		
Standard III		
Standard IV		
Standard V		
Standard VI		

RUBRIC FOR EXECUTIVE SUMMARY AND NARRATIVE DESCRIPTIONS/STANDARDS I–VI

Each evaluator will assess the narrative descriptions in two ways, using the rubrics below:

A. Ability to demonstrate acquisition and growth in Knowledge, Dispositions, and Performances for Standards I–VI.

B. Ability to articulate application of educational theories from credible educational researchers into practice for Standards I–VI.

A. Ability to Demonstrate Acquisition and Growth in Knowledge, Dispositions, and Performances

High	*Medium*	*Low*
Student provides several well-articulated, detailed examples of professional and/or personal growth in knowledge, skills, and attitudes throughout the length of his or her degree program.	Student provides some adequately articulated, detailed examples of professional and/or personal growth in knowledge, skills, and attitudes throughout the length of his or her degree program.	Student provides minimal poorly articulated examples of professional and/or personal growth in knowledge, skills, and attitudes throughout the length of his or her degree program.

B. Ability to Articulate Application of Educational Theories From Credible Educational Researchers Into Practice

3	*2*	*1*	*0*
Student provides multiple examples of applying research theories of prominent researchers to his or her practice.	Student provides some examples of applying research theories of prominent researchers to his or her practice.	Student provides few examples of applying research theories of prominent researchers to his or her practice.	Student provides no examples of applying research theories of prominent researchers to his or her practice.

Standard	*A. Ability to Demonstrate Acquisition and Growth in Knowledge, Dispositions, and Performances*	*B. Ability to Articulate Application of Educational Theories From Credible Educational Researchers Into Practice*
I		
II		
III		
IV		
V		
VI		
Executive Summary		

SOURCE: Used with permission of Trudy A. Salsberry, Teresa N. Miller, Mary Devin, and Robert J. Shoop.

Resource Q

Research Tracking Matrix

University-District Partnership Framework	*Leadership Standards*	*Standards for Leading Learning Communities*	*Research on Practice*	*Elements of Redesigned Preparation Programs*
A new vision of leadership practices; a blend of leadership theory and practice; a collaborative, restructured university and public school partnership; an integrated, spiraling-curriculum approach; a focus on ethics; long-term degree and/or licensure programs.	Interstate School Leaders Licensure Consortium *Standards for School Leaders* (ISLLC, 1996) developed by the Council of Chief State School Officers for the purpose of developing model standards to capture what is essential about the role of school leaders.	Six standards identified by National Association of Elementary School Principals (NAESP, 2001) for what principals should know and be able to do related to leading professional learning communities.	Twenty-one competencies that represent core understandings and capabilities required of successful principals, as identified by the National Policy Board for Educational Administration (NPBEA, 1993). Twenty-one responsibilities identified by McREL's meta-analysis (Waters & Grubb, 2004) to have significant relationship with student achievement. A systems orientation to the core technology of schooling by Leithwood, Aitken, and Jantzi (2006) identifies four broad categories of successful practices basic to leadership success in almost all situations.	Six strategies identified by Southern Regional Education Board (Bottoms, O'Neill, Fry, & Hill, 2003) for preparing a new breed of principals. Levine's (2005) nine-point template for judging the quality of school leadership programs.

References

Adams, C. M., & Pierce, R. L. (2006). Creative thinking. In F. A. Dixon & S. M. Moon (Eds.), *The handbook of secondary gifted education* (pp. 343–361). Waco, TX: Prufrock Press.

American Psychological Association. (2001). *Publication manual of the American Psychological Association* (5th ed.). Washington, DC: Author.

Bass, B. M. (1985). *Leadership and performance beyond expectations.* New York: Free Press.

Bass, B. M. (1990a). *Bass and Stogdill's handbook of leadership* (3rd ed.). New York: Free Press.

Bass, B. M. (1990b). From transactional to transformational leadership: Learning to share the vision. *Organizational Dynamics, 18*(3), 19–31.

Bass, B. M. (1997). The ethics of transformational leadership. *KLSP: Transformational Leadership Working Papers.* Maryland: Academy of Leadership Press. Retrieved April 2, 2007, from http://www.academy.umd.edu/publications/klspdocs/bbass_pl.htm

Bennis, W., & Biederman, P. (1997). *Organizing genius: The secret of creative collaboration.* Reading, MA: Addison-Wesley.

Bennis, W., & Goldsmith, J. (1997). *Learning to lead: A workbook on becoming a leader.* Reading, MA: Perseus.

Bennis, W., & Nanus, B. (1985). *Leaders: The strategies for taking charge.* New York: Harper & Row.

Bensimon, E. M. (1991). How college presidents use their administrative groups: Real and illusory teams. *Journal of Higher Education Management, 7,* 35–51.

Birnbaum, R. (1992). *How academic leadership works: Understanding success and failure in the college presidency.* San Francisco: Jossey-Bass.

Bottoms, G., O'Neill, K., Fry, B., & Hill, D. (2003). *Good principals are the key to successful schools: Six strategies to prepare more good principals.* Atlanta, GA: Southern Regional Education Board.

Burns, J. M. (1978). *Leadership.* New York: Harper & Row.

Champy, J. (2000, Summer). The residue of leadership: Why ambition matters. *Leader to Leader,* pp. 14–19.

Ciulla, J. B. (1995). *The ethics of leadership.* Belmont, CA: Wadsworth/Thompson.

Clouse, R. W., & Spurgeon, K. L. (1995). Corporate analysis of humor. *Psychology: A Quarterly Journal of Human Behavior, 32*(3/4), 1–24.

Collins, J. (2001). *Good to great: Why some companies make the leap . . . and others don't.* New York: HarperCollins.

Conzemius, A., & O'Neill , J. (2001). *Building shared responsibility for student learning.* Yorktown, VA: Virginia Association for Supervision and Curriculum.

Covey, S. R. (1989). *The 7 habits of highly effective people: Restoring the character ethic.* New York: Simon & Schuster.

Covey, S. R. (1992). *Principle-centered leadership.* New York: Summit Books.

Crawford, C. B. (1994). Theory and implications regarding the utilization of strategic humor by leaders. *Journal of Leadership Studies, 1,* 53–67.

Csikszentmihalyi, M. (1996). *Creativity: Flow and the psychology of discovery and invention.* New York: HarperCollins.

Devin, M. (2004). Save a place for leadership in the debate on adequacy: A new model for developing leadership for schools. *Educational Considerations, 32*(1), 70–75.

Dickmann, M. H., Stanford-Blair, N., & Rosati-Bojar, A. (2004). *Leading with the brain in mind: 101 brain-compatible practices for leaders.* Thousand Oaks, CA: Corwin Press.

Drucker, P. (1989). *The new realities.* New York: Harper & Row.

Drucker, P. (1991). The new productivity challenge. *Harvard Business Review, 69*(6), 72.

DuFour, R., Eaker, R., & DuFour, R. (2005). *On common ground: The power of professional learning communities.* Bloomington, IN: National Educational Service.

Duska, R., & Whelen, M. (1975). *Moral development: A guide to Piaget and Kohlberg.* New York: Paulist.

Elmore, R. (2000). *Building a new structure for school leadership.* Washington, DC: Albert Shanker Institute.

Fullan, M. (2005). *Leadership and sustainability: System thinkers in action.* Thousand Oaks, CA: Corwin Press.

Funk, R. C. (2005). *Evaluation of an academic program of leadership education.* Unpublished dissertation, Kansas State University, Manhattan.

Gardner, H. E. (1995). *Leading minds: An anatomy of leadership.* New York: Basic Books.

Gardner, J. W. (1990). *On leadership.* New York: Free Press.

Gellerman, S. W. (1986). Why "good" managers make bad ethical choices. *Harvard Business Review, 64*(4), 85–90.

Gilligan, C. (1982). *In a different voice: Psychological theory and women's development.* Cambridge, MA: Harvard University Press.

Goleman, D. (2006). *Social intelligence: The new science of social relationships.* New York: Random House.

Goleman, D., Boyatzis, R., & McKee, A. (2002). *Primal leadership.* Cambridge, MA: Harvard Business School Press.

Granirer, D. (2001). *Laughing your way to organizational health.* Retrieved October 28, 2006, from http://www.granirer.com/ART-0006.htm

Gunn, R. (2000). Can leadership be taught? *Strategic Finance, 82*(6), 14–17.

Gustafson, D. M. (2005). *A case study of a professional administrative leadership academy.* Unpublished doctoral dissertation, Kansas State University, Manhattan.

Hall, P. (2005, June). The principal's presence and supervision to improve teaching. *SEDL Letter,* pp. 26–16.

Harari, O. (1997, June). Looking beyond the vision thing. *Management Review,* pp. 26–29.

Heifetz, R. A. (1994). *Leadership without easy answers.* Cambridge, MA: Belknap Press.

Heifitz, R. A., & Linsky, M. (2002). *Leadership on the line.* Boston: Harvard Business School Press.

Henderson, N. (1998, January). Make resiliency happen. *Education Digest, 63,* 18.

Hof, R. D., Rebello, K., & Burrows, P. (1996, January 22). Scott McNealy's rising sun. *Business Week,* pp. 66–73.

Hogan, R., Curphy, G. J., & Hogan, J. (1994). What we know about leadership: Effectiveness and personality. *American Psychologist, 49,* 493–504.

Holmes, O. W. (2006). *Oliver Wendell Holmes quotes.* Retrieved October 28, 2006, from http://www.worldofquotes.com/author/Oliver-Wendell-Holmes/1/index.html

Iacocca, L. (2006). *Lee Iacocca quotes.* Retrieved October 28, 2006, from http://www.brainyquote.com/quotes/authors/1/lee_iacocca.html

Interstate School Leaders Licensure Consortium. (1996). *ISLLC standards for school leaders.* Washington, DC: Council of Chief State School Officers.

Ivory, G., & Acker-Hocevar, M. (2005). *Voices from the field: Phase 3* (Superintendent focus group interview transcripts). Austin, TX: University Council for Educational Administration.

Kansas Teachers Working Conditions Survey. (2006). Retrieved December 11, 2006, from http://www.kansastwc.org

Kennedy, J. F. K. (1961). *Inaugural address.* Retrieved July 1, 2006, from http://www.bartleby.com/124/pres56.html

Kidder, R. M. (1995). *How good people make tough choices.* New York: Simon & Schuster.

Kohlberg, L. (1984). *The psychology of moral development: The nature and validity of moral stages.* San Francisco: Harper & Row.

Kohlberg, L., & Hersh, R. H. (1977). Moral development: A review of the theory. *Theory Into Practice, 16*(2), 53–59.

Kouzes, J. M., & Posner, B. Z. (1993). *Credibility.* San Francisco: Jossey-Bass.

Kovalik, B. (with Olsen, K). (1994). *ITI: The model: Integrated thematic instruction* (3rd ed.). Washington, DC: Books for Educators.

Lambert, L. (2003). *Leadership capacity for lasting school improvement.* Yorktown, VA: Association for Supervision and Curriculum Development.

Leithwood, K., Aitken, R., & Jantzi, D. (2006). *Making schools smarter, third edition: Leading with evidence.* Thousand Oaks, CA: Corwin Press.

Leithwood, K., Louis, K. S., Anderson, S., & Wahlstrom, K. (2004). *How leadership influences student learning* (Executive summary). Minneapolis: University of Minnesota, Learning From Leadership Project of the Wallace Foundation.

Levine, A. (2005, March). *Educating school leaders.* New York: Education Schools Project.

Manasse, A. L. (1986). Vision and leadership: Paying attention to intention. *Peabody Journal of Education, 63*(1), 150–173.

Marzano, R., Waters, T., & McNulty, B. (2005). *School leadership that works: From research to results.* Yorktown, VA: Association for Supervision and Curriculum Development.

McLuhan, M. (2006). *Marshall McLuhan quotes.* Retrieved October 28, 2006, from http://www.en.thinkexist.com/quotes/marshall_mcluhan/

Miller, T., & Devin, M. (2005). *Academy evaluation transcripts.* Unpublished manuscript.

Miller, T. N., & Salsberry, T. (2005). Portfolio analysis: Documenting the progress and performance of educational administration students. *Educational Considerations, 33*(1), 29.

Murphy, J., & Vriesenga, M. (2004). *Research on preparation programs in educational administration: An analysis.* Columbia, MO: University Council for Educational Administration.

Murphy, J. T. (2006). Educating leaders for tomorrow's schools. *Phi Delta Kappan, 87,* 530–531, 536.

National Association of Elementary School Principals (NAESP). (2001). *Leading learning communities: NAESP standards for what principals should know and be able to do.* Alexandria, VA, and Washington, DC: NAESP and Collaborative Communications Group.

National Commission for Accrediting Teacher Education (NCATE). (2004). *Program review: Process.* Retrieved July 12, 2006, from http://www.ncate.org/institutions/process.asp

National Commission for Accrediting Teacher Education (NCATE). (2006). *Professional development school standards.* Retrieved October 28, 2006, from http://www.ncate.org/public/pdswhat.asp?ch-133

National Policy Board for Educational Administration (NPBEA). (1993). *Principals for our changing schools: Knowledge and skill base.* Fairfax, VA: Author.

No Child Left Behind Act of 2001, 20 U.S.C. 6301 et seq. (2002).

Pastor, J. (1996). Empowerment: What it is and what it is not. *Empowerment of Organizations, 4*(2), 5–7.

Paton, H. J. (1971). *The categorical imperative: A study in Kant's moral philosophy.* Philadelphia: University of Pennsylvania Press.

Patterson, J. (1993). *Leadership for tomorrow's schools.* Yorktown, VA: Association for Supervision and Curriculum Development.

Payne, R. (1996). *A framework for understanding poverty.* Highland, TX: aha! Process.

Peters, T. J. (1987). *Thriving on chaos: Handbook for a management revolution.* New York: Knopf.

Peters, T. J. (2000). Rule #3: Leadership is confusing as hell. *Fast Company Magazine, 44,* 124. Retrieved June 23, 2006, from http://www.fastcompany.com/online/44/rules.html

Pickens, T. B. (2006). *T. Boone Pickens quotes.* Retrieved October 28, 2006, from http://www.brainyquote.com/quotes/authors/t/t_boone_pickens.html

Portin, B., Schneider, P., DeArmond, M., & Gundlach, L. (2003). *Making sense of leading schools: A study of the school principalship.* Washington, DC: Center on Reinventing Public Education.

Reeves, D. B. (2006). *The learning leader: How to focus school improvement for better results.* Yorktown, VA: Association for Supervision and Curriculum Development.

Rest, J. R., & Narvaez, P. (1994). *Moral development in the professions.* Hillsdale, NJ: Lawrence Erlbaum.

Roosevelt, T. (2006). *Theodore Roosevelt quotes.* Retrieved October 28, 2006, from http://www.brainyquote.com/quotes/authors/t/theodore_roosevelt.html

Rost, J. (1991). *Leadership for the 21st century.* New York: Praeger.

Schmoker, M. (2005, June). The new fundamentals of leadership. *SEDL Letter,* pp. 3–7.

Senge, P. M. (1990). *The fifth discipline.* New York: Doubleday.

Sergiovanni, T. J. (1990). Adding value to leadership gets extraordinary results. *Education Leadership, 47*(8), 23–27.

Spillane, J. (2006). *Distributed leadership.* San Francisco: Jossey-Bass.
Stone, D., Patton, B., & Heen, S. (1999). *Difficult conversations: How to discuss what matters most.* New York: Viking Press.
Sultanoff, S. M. (1993). *Taking humor seriously in the workplace.* Retrieved May 23, 2006, from http://humormatters.com/articles/workplac.htm
Tenbrunsel, A. E., & Messick, D. M. (2004). Ethical fading: The role of self-deception in unethical behavior. *Social Justice Research, 17,* 223–236.
Tichy, N. (with Cohen, E.). (1998). *The leadership engine: Building leaders at every level.* Dallas, TX: Pritchett & Associates.
Treffinger, D. J., & Isaksen, S. G. (1992). *Creative problem solving: An introduction.* Sarasota, FL: Center for Creative Learning.
Waters, T., & Grubb, S. (2004). *The leadership we need: Using research to strengthen the use of standards for administrator preparation and licensure programs.* Aurora, CO: McREL.
Waters, T., Marzano, R. J., & McNulty, B. (2003). *Balanced leadership: What 30 years of research tells us about the effect of leadership on student achievement.* Aurora, CO: McREL.
Weber, M. (1946). *The theory of social and economic organizations* (T. Parsons, Ed.; A. M. Henderson & T. Parsons, Trans.). New York: Free Press.
Werner, E. E., & Smith, R. S. (1982). *Vulnerable but invincible: A longitudinal study of resilient children and youth.* New York: McGraw-Hill.
Wheatley, M. (1997, Summer). Goodbye, command and control. *Leader to Leader, 5,* 21–28.
Whitney, W. R. (2006). *Willis R. Whitney quotes.* Retrieved October 28, 2006, from http://quotes.zaadz.com/Willis_R_Whitney
Wolf, G. (1996, February). Steve Jobs: The next insanely great thing. *Wired News,* Issue 4.02. Retrieved May 23, 1996, from http://www.wired.com/wired/archive/4.02/jobs_pr.html
York-Barr, J., Sommers, W. A., Ghere, G. S., & Montie, J. (2006). *Reflective practice to improve schools: An action guide for educators.* Thousand Oaks, CA: Corwin Press.
Zacharakis, J., Devin, M., & Miller, T. (2006, April 10). *Leadership characteristics of public school superintendents in Kansas.* Paper presented at American Educational Research Association Annual Meeting, San Francisco.

WEB RESOURCES

Center for Teaching Quality, Chapel Hill, NC: http://www.teachingquality.org
Kansas Teachers Working Conditions Survey 2006 results: http://www.Kansastwc.org
McREL. *Asking the Right Questions Toolkit:* http://www.mcrel.org/toolkit
Southern Regional Education Board (SREB). (2006). *Schools can't wait: Accelerating the redesign of university principal preparation programs:* http://www.sreb.org

Index

The Corwin Press logo—a raven striding across an open book—represents the union of courage and learning. Corwin Press is committed to improving education for all learners by publishing books and other professional development resources for those serving the field of PreK–12 education. By providing practical, hands-on materials, Corwin Press continues to carry out the promise of its motto: **"Helping Educators Do Their Work Better."**

The American Association of School Administrators, founded in 1865, is the professional organization for over 13,000 educational leaders across America and in many other countries. AASA's mission is to support and develop effective school system leaders who are dedicated to the highest quality public education for all children.